BASIC PERSONAL COUNSELLING

A training manual for counsellors

David Geldard

Illustrated by Garry Anderson

PRENTICE HALL

New York   London   Toronto   Sydney   Tokyo

Typeset by: Midnight Express Professional Typesetting Pty Ltd, Cromer, N.S.W.

Printed and bound in Australia by: Macarthur Press Sales Pty Ltd, Parramatta, NSW.

Cover design by Garry Anderson

2 3 4 5 93 92 91 90
ISBN 0 7248 0094 8

**National Library of Australia
Cataloguing-in-Publication Data**

Geldard, David.
    Basic personal counselling.

    Bibliography.
    Includes index.
    ISBN 0 7248 0094 8.

    1. Counseling.   I. Title.

158'.3

Prentice Hall, Inc., *Englewood Cliffs, New Jersey*
Prentice Hall Canada, Inc., *Toronto*
Prentice Hall Hispanoamericana, SA, *Mexico*
Prentice Hall of India Private Ltd, *New Delhi*
Prentice Hall International, Inc., *London*
Prentice Hall of Japan, Inc., *Tokyo*
Prentice Hall of Southeast Asia Pty Ltd, *Singapore*
Editora Prentice Hall do Brasil Ltda, *Rio de Janeiro*

PRENTICE HALL

A division of Simon & Schuster

Contents

Part V   Counselling practicalities

Part VI   The counsellor's own needs

Acknowledgments

Sincere thanks go to:

Mrs Sandra Magnus, who typed the manuscript, gave continual encouragement, and made many helpful suggestions. Without her persistence and friendship this book may never have been completed;

My daughter, Alison, for editing and improving the original manuscript;

Past and present colleagues, at Lifeline Brisbane, for their friendship and interest in this project;

Dr Peter Mulholland, Dr Arlene Morgan, Rev. Ross Waters and Rev. Dr Charles Noller, for their contributions to my personal and professional development;

Lifeline Brisbane and Margaret Hegarty for permission to use the transcript of a counselling session illustrating paraphrasing;

Dr Lisa Gaffney for her help with regard to my understanding and research in the area of burnout.

PART I
Counselling

1 Becoming a counsellor

To you, the reader, I say "Welcome".

Firstly, let me introduce myself by telling you who I am. My name is David, and it fits me well. I am 52 years old, and am a proud father and grandfather. My work is a large part of me. I am a full-time counsellor in a crisis counselling agency, and after some years working as a personal counsellor, I now specialize in family therapy. My work allows me to be creative and to use myself as a person. Generally it is stimulating and satisfying, but at times it is stressful and can be exhausting.

I believe in sexual equality and am aware, as I write this book, that I am a male, and that however hard I try, what I write will inevitably be written from a male perspective. Please allow for this if you find that for you, what I have written, does not always fit. There are clients and counsellors of both sexes, and one way of writing would be to use combined personal pronouns such as she/he. However, I do not like that approach because it is not consistent with our spoken language and spoils the flow of the written word. I will therefore write half the chapters in this book using the female gender predominantly (she, her), and the other half using the male gender predominantly (he, his).

I hope you will enjoy reading this book and find it useful. Because you are reading it, my guess is that you are either intending to train as a counsellor, or are concerned with training other people to be counsellors. I am writing primarily for the trainee, and as I write I remember how I felt when I first started my training. My feelings and attitudes then were very different from those which I have now. However, it was those feelings and attitudes which motivated me to go ahead. I wonder how you feel as you think about your decision to train as a counsellor? What are your motivations? Stop for a minute and think. Ask yourself the question, "Why do I want to be a counsellor?" and, if you have the energy, write your answer on a sheet of paper so that you can refer to it later.

Your answer is, of course, individually yours, but it is quite probable that it fits into one of two possible moulds. It could be that you wrote a statement about your *own* needs. Maybe you have the idea that being a counsellor will give you status, power or satisfaction. Perhaps you think that counselling will add a new quality and richness to your life. It may be though that when you wrote your answer you were not thinking about your own needs at all. You may have decided to become a counsellor so that you can satisfy the needs of other people. You may have written down something like "I want to be a counsellor because I care about others and want to help them". Most counsellors are very caring people and helping others is an important part of their motivation. However it's important for you to remember that even if you become a counsellor with the primary goal of satisfying other people's needs, then you will *also* be satisfying some of your *own* needs too. You will, for example, get satisfaction for yourself out of caring for others. This discussion may not seem important to you right now, but it is, because your motivation for becoming a counsellor will, if you are not careful, heavily influence the way in which you will function as a counsellor. While it probably doesn't matter greatly what your motivation is, it is important that you are aware of your motivation and of what needs of your own you hope to satisfy. With this awareness you will be better able to avoid letting the satisfaction of your own needs interfere with the counselling process, and with your ability to meet the needs of clients.

In order to be able to meet the needs of clients a counsellor must have an understanding of the purposes and goals of the counselling process. If I am to become an effective counsellor, then I need to have some idea of what it means to be effective. Judging the effectiveness of counselling is usually subjective and there are clearly two different perspectives—the client's and the counsellor's. It may be that the client will perceive effectiveness in a different way from the counsellor, so I am asking you, the reader, to spend a few minutes looking first at the client's expectations and then at the counsellor's.

To understand the client's perspective it is probably useful to look at the reasons why clients seek counselling. For most people it is not easy to make an appointment and then go to see a counsellor. Our society's value system holds that it's a sign of weakness if people are unable to handle their problems without outside help. This tends to make it difficult for those with heavy work responsibilities to come for counselling. Such people often believe that their colleagues would think that they were inadequate and not capable of taking responsibility, if they admitted to seeking help from a counsellor. Consequently, many people are reluctant to seek counselling unless they are in such a disturbed emotional state that their ability to carry out their normal daily tasks is significantly impaired, and they are no longer able to hide their pain and emotional distress from others.

Often, a client will go to a counsellor with very unrealistic expectations of what is likely to happen in the counselling session. Frequently a client will expect that the counsellor will give her direct advice, and tell her exactly what to do, so that at the end of the session she can go away having solved her problems. Most counsellors would agree that they are not prepared to meet such client expectations. Moreover, there are real disadvantages to

the client if the counsellor does try to give advice and provide solutions to problems.

There are several dangers inherent in giving advice. Firstly, human beings are remarkably resistant to advice. In fact, some counsellors have become so impressed by the way that clients resist advice, that in advanced counselling sessions, paradoxical methods are sometimes used where a client is advised to do exactly the reverse of what the counsellor really wants her to do! Other counsellors do give direct advice but this may be counter-productive even if the client follows the advice. If the advice turns out to be inappropriate, then quite clearly the counsellor has done the client a disservice and she will not be impressed. On the other hand, if the advice has positive consequences for the client then unfortunately there may still be negative consequences in the long term. Instead of working things out for herself, the client has accepted the counsellor's advice and may now regard the counsellor as a superior expert who needs to be consulted whenever major decisions are to be made. This is clearly undesirable, and suggests that an important goal for a counsellor may be to teach or encourage the client to become self-reliant and to feel confident about her own ability to make decisions. In the long term it is not helpful for a client to become dependent on a counsellor's advice. It is far better for the client to become self-reliant, and capable of making and trusting her own decisions.

If I am to be an effective counsellor, I need to have a clear idea of my goals. One of my own primary goals is to help the client to feel better, or at least to feel more comfortable, particularly in the long term. It is also my aim to help a client learn how to become more self-sufficient, and how to deal with ongoing and future life situations in a constructive way without requiring continual help. It is very much in both the client's and the counsellor's interests to promote enduring long-term change, rather than to engage in short-term problem solving. A counsellor is clearly going to feel very frustrated if clients keep returning for counselling each time new problems are encountered. It is important, if the counsellor is to feel a sense of satisfaction in her work, that clients change and grow in such a way that they learn to cope, as much as is realistically possible, on their own.

Another desirable counselling goal is to bring about change as quickly as is possible in a client. Clearly a counsellor might be seen to be more effective if change is produced more quickly. However, be aware of the danger of producing short-term transitory change which is not sustainable, and fails to enable the client to cope more effectively with future crises.

As discussed above, there may often be a mismatch between a client's expectations and the counsellor's goals. There are a number of ways of dealing with this mismatch. One way, of course, would be to ignore it and just to allow the counselling process to proceed. Some counsellors do this.

However, an alternative approach is to openly discuss expectations with the client and to formalize a counselling contract which is mutually acceptable to both.

In summary, most counsellors don't give advice, don't "problem solve" and don't seek to produce quick short-term solutions without long-term gain. Instead they help clients sort out their own confusion, and by doing this enable them to discover for themselves solutions to their problems which fit for them. Often the counsellor may think that these solutions are not the most sensible or appropriate ones. However, it is important for a client to make decisions which are right for her. She can then test her decisions and learn from her own experiences, rather than learning to rely on the "wisdom" of the counsellor.

There are many different styles of counselling. Although this book uses ideas from various therapies such as Gestalt Therapy, Rational Emotive Therapy, and Neuro Linguistic Programming, the underlying emphasis throughout is on the non-directive counselling style originated by Carl Rogers. This is a useful style for beginners to adopt because it provides a good foundation on which to build by adding advanced skills which are beyond the scope of this book. The style described is also relatively safe because an inexperienced counsellor is less likely to damage a client by using this approach than by using other methods.

The key to helping a client work effectively through her problems and sort out her confusion lies in the client–counsellor relationship. Indeed, research seems to demonstrate that it doesn't matter greatly what style of counselling a counsellor uses provided that the relationship between the client and counsellor is one which is appropriate for producing therapeutic change.

2 The counselling relationship

For me, learning to become an effective counsellor was a long process during which I discovered and absorbed ideas about counselling from my own practical experience, and through contact with my supervisors, other counsellors, clients and friends. It is those ideas which I am sharing with you. Very little of what you will read here has been learnt by me from my own reading. Most of it has been learnt through the experience of being a client myself, being a trainee and then a counsellor, and through talking with people who are counsellors or who have been counselled. I have learnt more by experience than by reading. I hope that you too will put a higher value on your own personal experience than on what you read.

Although Carl Rogers' book *Client-Centred Therapy* was first published years ago, its ideas are still relevant today. Rogers' concept of the counselling relationship is both powerful and useful, and needs to be understood by the trainee counsellor. Once a Rogerian counselling style has been developed then additional skills may be learnt and incorporated into your counselling repertoire.

Carl Rogers identified three basic qualities which are highly desirable for a counsellor if counselling is to be effective. These qualities are congruence, empathy, and unconditional positive regard. I will describe these qualities in the following paragraphs.

Congruence

To be congruent the counsellor must be genuinely himself, a complete, integrated and whole person. Everything about him must ring true. Let me use myself as an example. There is only one David Geldard even though I have a variety of roles. I am a father, a counsellor, a friend, a brother, a patient, a customer etc. It is clearly true that there are differences in the way that I behave in each of these roles, and in different situations. While I'm playing with a child I am happy to romp around on the floor, and when I'm attending a professional meeting of psychologists I prefer to dress more formally and sit upright on a chair. However, in both situations I have a choice. I can if I choose be an actor playing a role or I can in the fullest sense really be me. I can either stay fully in contact with myself as a person and be genuine, without the need to change myself, or if I choose I can disown myself, wear a mask, and pretend to be different from the real me. As a counsellor I could, for example, pretend to be an expert who has all the answers and no vulnerabilities, or I can throw away my "counsellor mask" and just be me, the real person complete with all my strengths and weaknesses. When a client comes to see me in my counsellor role, then two people meet. It is a person-to-person relationship. For the client to feel valued, I, the counsellor, need to be congruently myself, genuine in all regards. If this happens, then the relationship will be enhanced and the counselling process is likely to be more effective.

Each time I enter a counselling relationship I bring with me that part of me which is a parent, that part of me which is a professional psychologist, that part of me which is childlike and likes to have fun and play jokes on people, and the serious side of me. I also bring with me some spiritual beliefs and some doubts about those spiritual beliefs. I am very much me and not just part of me. I am, within my own limitations, genuinely me and do not pretend to be different from the real me, and I am OK (Satir, 1975). Naturally, when working as a counsellor I make use of those parts of me that are most relevant in the counselling relationship, and other parts of me may remain out of sight. These are not deliberately concealed from the client, but are available if they can be appropriately used.

I ran a group recently, and in that group were two of my personal friends. These two people had never seen me as a counsellor but had only known me as a friend. After the group, one of them said to me, "I was really surprised because in the group you were the therapist, but all I saw was the person that I had always known, and I expected to find someone different". A similar situation occurred when a lecturer friend of mine at our local university was teaching counselling skills. One of the students, early on in the course, said to the lecturer, "How about you show us how you counsel by giving us a demonstration. You've been teaching us these micro-skills, but you've never actually sat down in front of us and demonstrated how to counsel". The lecturer readily agreed, sat down and as counsellor, helped a young student client to resolve a difficult and painful issue. After the session was over, the student who'd asked the lecturer to give the demonstration seemed to be amazed and delighted. She said to the lecturer, "You know, I really can't believe it. It was just as though you were being yourself, and Irene (invented name) and you were talking together like friends". Yes, that's how it was, the lecturer was being totally congruent and was relating to Irene as she related to other people in her daily life, as a real person. Of course, it wasn't quite the same, because in daily life we generally behave as though our own needs are equally as important as other people's needs, whereas in a counselling relationship the counsellor will generally focus on the client's needs rather than his own. After all, the counselling situation is not the appropriate place for a counsellor to work through his own problems; rather it's the place where the central focus is the client.

Empathy

When a client is talking I imagine that he is walking along a path. Sometimes he meanders away from the path, goes into the woods, trips over, climbs over rocks, wanders through valleys, crosses streams and generally explores. Sometimes he goes right around in a circle and comes back to the same point again. As a counsellor I am neither a follower nor a leader most of the time, although at times I will follow and at times I will lead. Most of the time, what I try to do is to walk alongside the client—to go where he chooses to go, to explore those things that he chooses to explore, and to be warm, open, friendly, concerned, caring, real and genuine. This way trust develops between the client and myself and I experience the world in almost the same way that he experiences it. I try to think and feel the way the client does, so that I can share with him what he is discovering about himself. I go on a journey with him, hand-in-hand, listening to everything he says, matching his every move, being right beside him. This is what is meant by empathy. Being empathic means having a togetherness with the client, and as a consequence creating a trusting environment in which he feels cared for and safe. In such an environment the client can talk about his darkest secrets, his innermost feelings, and the things that seem to him to be so terrible, or so personal that he does not dare to talk to others about them.

Unconditional positive regard

The third counsellor characteristic essential for effective counselling is unconditional positive regard. Unconditional positive regard involves accepting the client completely, in a non-judgmental way, as the person that he is, with all his frailties and weaknesses, and with all his strengths and positive qualities. Having unconditional positive regard doesn't mean that I agree with or accept the values of the client for myself, but it does mean that I accept the client as he is now, value him as a person, am non-judgmental of his behaviour, and do not try to put my values onto him. I consequently enable him to feel free to be open in exploring his inner processes without censoring them for fear of criticism. This gives him the best opportunity for increased personal awareness and consequent growth.

Unconditional positive regard isn't always easy to achieve. The first step in attempting to achieve it is to try to see the world through the eyes of the client. By doing this I am better able to understand the client's motivations

for his behaviour and to be more accepting of that behaviour. The longer I've been a counsellor, the more convinced I have become that even the most terrible behaviour is often understandable if I first understand the world that the client lives in and has lived in. I take the view that inside every person, behind the facade that the world sees, there is somebody who has the potential to be a good, creative, loving person. I am rarely disappointed by this expectation.

By caring for each person who talks with me in the same way that I care for myself, I am better able to be accepting and non-judgmental. I'm not going to pretend that this is easy, because it often isn't, and sometimes in a counselling room I hear things that seem at first to be quite outrageous and terrible. At these times, it is really hard for me to be non-judgmental, but it is a goal that I strive for. Only by being non-judgmental can I earn the total trust of the client and really see the world in the way he does. Only then am I able to facilitate change effectively.

Clearly, being non-judgmental and accepting clients with unconditional positive regard is not easily achieved. Moreover it will be very difficult for me to create the relationship I need to have with a client and to be non-judgmental unless first I am very clear about who I am and what my own values are. If I have not sorted out my own value conflicts, then there is a risk that my own confusion will interfere with my ability to focus on the client's confusion, and I may inadvertently end up using the counselling session to resolve my own conflicts rather than the client's. To get a better understanding of my own values I have had to explore them, to scrutinize them and to question them. I have needed to carefully consider different values from my own and to understand where my feelings about those different values come from. This is an ongoing process which will never be finished until I die. I have found that often when I have had extremely polarized views, this has been because I have been afraid to look at the opposite point of view and to understand it. Through sorting out my own value system, understanding myself better, and consequently being less threatened by views which are diametrically opposed to mine, I am better able to take a non-judgmental attitude towards clients who have very different value systems from mine.

In this chapter I have discussed the counselling relationship, and have explained how that relationship is important in providing a trusting, caring, environment in which the client will feel free to share with the counsellor in the most open way possible. The attributes of congruence, genuineness, warmth, empathy and unconditional positive regard are extremely important if a counsellor is to be fully effective. A counsellor needs to walk alongside the client and to be with him in a very real sense so that the client experiences a togetherness. The precise words the counsellor uses are less important than his ability to form a meaningful relationship with the client and to listen intently to what his client is saying. An effective counsellor listens more than he talks, and what he does say confirms for the client that he is being heard and understood. The counsellor's role involves helping the client to explore his world and so to sort out his confusion. It is not the counsellor's role to choose the direction in which the client moves, but rather to provide the environment in which the client can best decide where to go. The counsellor then accompanies him on his journey of exploration. As a counsellor, allow your client to go where his current energy is taking him rather than trying to lead him in a particular direction. When the client has learnt to trust you, and to know that you will listen to the trivial, then he will feel safe enough to venture towards the real source of his pain. In other words, if you stay with the trivial the important will emerge.

You may by now have come to the conclusion that counselling is a terribly serious process. It often is. It is also a process that can give a great deal of satisfaction to the counsellor, and there are even times when counselling can be fun. Is there any fun in you? There certainly is in me, and I enjoy bringing my sense of humour into the therapeutic environment when that is appropriate. Don't fall into the trap of thinking that counselling is always a deadpan, heavy and serious process. It isn't. I am a real person and I need to be congruent. I need to be able to bring all of me into the counselling relationship, and to use those parts of my personality which can add richness to the therapeutic encounter whenever possible.

3 An overview of skills training

Micro-skills and methods of learning

You can't learn to be a counsellor by reading a book. "Oh . . . !" I can hear you saying. "I've just wasted my money buying this training manual." My belief is that if you intend to use this manual alone, then it will be of limited value, but that if you use this book in conjunction with practical training, then you will find it really useful. There are two components involved in learning to become a counsellor. One is understanding what counselling is about and how you are going to do it—in other words to have a theoretical framework from which to operate. The other component is to obtain practical skills training under the supervision of a competent counsellor and trainer. I doubt whether it is possible to learn counselling in any other way. My assumption is that you are reading this book to gain an understanding of basic counselling principles, and that at the same time you are undergoing a practical course of training.

Many people have the idea that counselling requires a great deal of skill and is something rather difficult and complicated to learn. If that is what you believe, then stop and ask yourself a few questions. Have you ever comforted a child who was crying? Have you ever spent time sitting quietly with a friend who was terribly upset? Have you ever listened to somebody who was in a dilemma, and who did not know what to do? My guess is that you have done all of these things, and that you have on many occasions in your life acted in a natural way as a counsellor with a friend, a relative, a child or maybe even with someone that you met casually. What was the most important thing that you did in these situations? Was it just to let the person know that you cared enough about her to listen to her problem and to be with her in her distress? If it was, then you were behaving like a counsellor. Counselling is an extension of what we all do naturally in our relationships with others when they are hurting. From your own experience you will know that some people are more gifted than others at counselling in a natural way. We all know people who are such good listeners that their friends frequently talk over problems with them. Such people are natural counsellors. The aim of counsellor training, is to help you to improve your natural counselling skills, and so to become more effective in helping others to deal with their pain.

15

In the previous chapter we considered the importance of the counselling relationship. Certainly the relationship is central in counselling, but there are a number of individual skills which can be learnt which greatly enhance the quality and effectiveness of the counselling relationship. Techniques used by counsellors have been analyzed and broken down into small elements of counselling behaviour known as micro-skills. Each of the micro-skills can be learnt individually. However, be warned: a trainee needs to remember that counselling competence seems to initially diminish after each input of micro-skill training. This is because the trainee inevitably concentrates on using the new skill, rather than on building and maintaining the relationship. Also, the trainee isn't able to behave naturally when using a new skill until that skill is fully mastered. Once the skill is fully mastered it becomes a natural part of the counsellor's way of relating, and counselling effectiveness is considerably increased.

In the following chapters, each of the micro-skills will be explained, one by one. After reading each chapter, it will be best if you practise the relevant micro-skill in a group setting. The usual way to do this is in a triad or a group of three students. One student takes the role of counsellor, a second student takes the role of client and the third student takes the role of observer. Here are some suggestions about how to work in triads. If you are training for face-to-face counselling, set the room up with the chairs facing each other as shown in Figure 1, so that the "client" faces the "counsellor" and the observer watches both.

Telephone counselling is rather different from face-to-face counselling because the telephone counsellor can't see the caller who is her client. Consequently the counsellor doesn't have any visual indication of the client's non-verbal behaviour. The chairs for triad practice for trainee telephone counsellors should therefore be set out with the "counsellor" chair and the

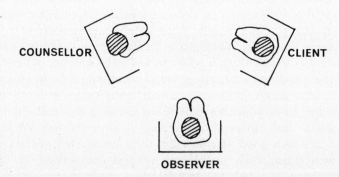

Figure 1.   Chair arrangement for face-to-face counselling practice.

"client" chair in a back-to-back arrangement as shown in Figure 2, so that the "counsellor" and "client" cannot see each other. However the observer's chair should face the other two chairs so that the observer is aware of what is happening non-verbally, and can feed this back to the other two students at the end of each practice session.

It is very important that the "client" in the triad should present a current and real personal problem of her own. Sometimes I have met students who have told me quite emphatically that they did not have such a thing as a personal problem, and I have found that difficult to believe. I doubt whether such people really exist. In my experience, whenever people have said to me that they don't have any personal problems, I have discovered later that there have been areas of their lives which they were unwilling to discuss, and which they had blocked off and were afraid to venture near. Their fear was often related to a lack of trust in other members of the triad and to feelings of vulnerability associated with self-disclosure. Unfortunately trainee counsellors frequently believe that they will not be accepted as counsellors if they disclose problems of their own. Trainees have often asked me whether they can use invented problems or other people's problems, but in my view this is not satisfactory. Most people who have been involved as trainers of counsellors would agree that it is much easier for the student counsellor to respond in a real and genuine way to what is being said if the problem is real, and not invented or borrowed from someone else. Whenever a make-believe problem is used, it is difficult for the trainee counsellor to accurately pick up the "client's" feelings and to appropriately practise counselling skills.

The "counsellor" in a counselling triad should listen, and practise only those micro-skills which have been taught so far and not use any other type of response at all. This may seem to be very limiting, but in fact it is possible to carry out an effective counselling session by using only one or two micro-

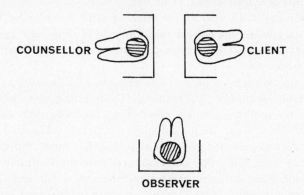

Figure 2. Chair arrangement for telephone counselling practice.

skills on their own. In Chapter 5 there is a transcript of a counselling session where I was the client and an experienced counsellor counselled me. That particular counselling session was useful to me as the client, in helping me to resolve a problem that had become quite troublesome, and it is interesting to note that the counsellor used only two micro-skills and did not use any other type of response.

The observer's role in the triad is to take notes of anything significant which she observes during the counselling practice session. The observer does not make judgments about what should have been done, but rather has the task of observing, as objectively as possible, and without making interpretations, what actually happens during the practice session. This information is fed back to the "counsellor" and "client" at the end of the session.

Practice counselling sessions should typically be short, of about ten minutes' length, and at the end of each session the observer should share her observations with the other two members of the triad. After that, the "client" should be given the opportunity to talk about how she felt during the counselling session, and finally the "counsellor" should explore her own feelings, and share with the group how the session was for her. Preferably, in addition to the student observer there should be an experienced trainer observing the triad throughout, but in large group counsellor training, it frequently happens that trainers have to go from triad to triad and are only able to spend a short time with each small group.

Before working in a triad, the skill that is to be practised should be modelled by a competent counsellor. There are two ways in which this can be done. Either the demonstration can be performed live, or a video recording may be used. My favoured option is the video-recorded demonstration, because too often live demonstrations, even with competent counsellors, include segments of inappropriate modelling.

This chapter has dealt with an overview of skills training for beginners with no previous counselling experience. Once basic skills have been learnt, the trainee counsellor needs to have ongoing training with real clients as discussed in Chapter 26.

The following chapters on micro-skills have been deliberately arranged in the most suitable sequence for training. By learning the skills in this sequence, the trainee can practise counselling by using only one or two micro-skills initially, and can then gradually incorporate additional skills into her repertoire. The sequence given is such that the most important basic skills are learnt first, with the consequence that more practice will be obtained in using these skills and the trainee counsellor will begin to rely on them as being the ones which are most appropriate for frequent use.

PART II
Micro-skills

4 Attending to the clien
and the use of
minimal responses

Although clients often ask for advice, they generally don't like being given advice, and rarely, if ever, go to a counsellor to listen to the counsellor. They go to counsellors to do the talking themselves, to get things off their chests, to ventilate their feelings, and to say the things that would be very difficult or maybe impossible to say to friends or family. If you can remember that the client has really come to talk to you and to unload on to you the stuff that is troubling him, and that he has not come to listen to *you* talking to *him*, then you will have a better understanding of the counselling relationship.

A counsellor is primarily a listener. By listening to what the client says, the counsellor is able to help him to sort through his confusion and muddle, identify his dilemmas, explore his options, and come away from the counselling session feeling that something useful has occurred. The counsellor therefore needs to attend very carefully to everything that the client is saying and to remember the smallest details of the conversation. If you want to convince your client that you really are listening, then you won't need to ask him the names of his relatives a second time. You won't need to ask him to remind you of what happened five years ago in his relationships, or about something trivial that he hardly mentioned. You will remember these details, because during the counselling session you will be focusing your concentration on the client and on what he is telling you. A good way of letting him know that he has your full attention is by use of the minimal response.

The minimal response is something that we automatically do in our conversation when we are predominantly listening rather than talking. Counselling involves the art of listening constructively and so appropriate use of the minimal response is essential. Minimal responses are sometimes non-verbal and include just a nod of the head. Also included among minimal responses are expressions like, "A-ha", "Uh-hm", "Yes", "OK", and "Right". While the client is talking continuously, the counsellor needs from time to time to reaffirm that he is listening to what the client is saying, and this can be done by inserting minimal responses at regular intervals.

Chapter 4

As a counsellor, space your minimal responses appropriately. If they are given too frequently, then they will become intrusive and will be distracting. Conversely, if they are not included frequently enough the client may believe that you are not really attending to what he is saying. Additionally, in order to create an empathic relationship, match the speed of talking and tone of voice of your client. When he talks rapidly respond similarly, and when he slows up be more leisurely yourself.

The minimal response is not just an acknowledgement that the client is being heard. It can also be a subtle way of communicating other messages. It may be used to signify that the counsellor agrees with the client, or to emphasize the importance of a client statement, to express surprise, or even to query the appropriateness of what the client is saying. The way in which a minimal response is given—the tone of voice used, the accompanying non-verbal behaviour such as eye movements, facial expressions and body posture—all combine to convey a message to the client.

Some longer responses serve a similar function to the minimal response. For example, the counsellor might say "I hear what you say", or "I understand". Along with the use of minimal responses, another way in which a counsellor can help the client to feel that he is really being listened to is to match his non-verbal behaviour. If a client is sitting on the edge of the seat, with his arms on his knees looking forwards, then it may be useful for the counsellor to sit in the same way and in effect to mirror the client's posture. By doing this, the client is likely to feel as though there is some intimacy between himself and the counsellor, rather than that the counsellor is a superior expert sitting back, listening and judging what is being said. Similarly, if the client leans back in his chair with his legs crossed, and the counsellor casually matches that posture, the client may well feel more at ease.

If the counsellor matches the client's non-verbal behaviour and posture for a while, then more often than not the client will match the counsellor's behaviour when the counsellor makes a change. In this way the counsellor may bring about a change in the client's emotional state. For example, by matching the speed and tone of speaking and the speed of breathing of an agitated client, the counsellor joins with him. When the counsellor wants to do so, he can slow down his breathing, his speaking speed, and can sit back comfortably in his chair. If the matching has been done effectively, then it is highly likely that the client will follow the counsellor's example and will also slow down and adopt a more relaxed posture. This technique can be very helpful at certain stages of the counselling process.

The counsellor should be careful not to move his body too quickly during a counselling session, as this can distract a client and interrupt his train of thought. However, the counsellor needs to be relaxed, and should feel free to move his position in a natural way whenever he wants, but this should be done slowly and not suddenly.

Eye contact is also important in establishing rapport with the client. In the past, some counsellors believed that eye contact should be continuous, and that the counsellor should look continuously into the eyes of the client. This is a very unnatural thing to do and might lead to an eyeball contest, where the client feels uncomfortably stared at rather than joined with. Clearly the counsellor needs to maintain a good level of eye contact with the client, and to observe the normal social conventions by behaving naturally in allowing himself to look away from time to time.

As a new counsellor, I remember often not focusing fully on what the client was saying, but instead rehearsing my next counselling response. That behaviour on my part was really destructive to the counselling process. It was due to my nervousness and desire to appear to be professional and competent rather than friendly and real. Also I was uncomfortable with silence and felt that I had a responsibility to fill up the gaps in the conversation. Now I am more comfortable with silence and there is no pressure on me to give a response the instant that the client stops talking. Instead I feel relaxed enough to allow the client, if he wants to, to think in silence. Often when a client has just finished making a very powerful and personal statement, he will need time to sit silently and process what he has said. Match the client's silence whilst continuing to pay attention to him with appropriate eye contact. If you observe his eye movements carefully, you will be able to tell when he is thinking and needs to be left to think rather than to be interrupted. Whilst thinking, the client's eyes are likely to be focused steadily at a distance and when he has stopped thinking his eyes will tell you.

5 Reflection of content (paraphrasing)

As explained in the previous chapter, the primary function of the counsellor is to actively listen so that the client believes with confidence that she is being both heard and understood. However, it's obvious that just attending to the client by matching non-verbal behaviour and giving minimal responses is not sufficient. The counsellor also needs to respond more actively, and by doing so to draw out the really important content details of what the client is saying and to clarify those for the client. The most common and generally most effective way of doing this is by using the skill called *paraphrasing* or *reflection of content*. Using this skill the counsellor literally reflects back to the client what the client has said to the counsellor. The counsellor does not just parrot or repeat word for word what the client has said but instead paraphrases it. This means that the counsellor picks out the most important content details of what the client has said and re-expresses them in a clearer way, if that is possible, and in her own words rather than in the client's. The following are some examples of paraphrasing to help you understand how the skill is used.

Examples of paraphrasing or reflection of content

Example 1
CLIENT STATEMENT: I'm fighting with my daughter, my husband's not speaking to me, at work the boss keeps picking on me, and what's more my best friend doesn't seem to understand me any more.
COUNSELLOR RESPONSE: You're having a lot of relationship problems.

Example 2
CLIENT STATEMENT: I spent all day Saturday cleaning up my girlfriend's yard but she was annoyed because she said I'd cut the shrubs too short, I'd over-pruned them. Then I went to a great deal of trouble repainting the back door. Once again she didn't like the colour. Finally I suggested that she might go out to eat with me and would you believe when she got to the restaurant she decided that she really didn't like that restaurant at all. I keep trying to think of things that she would like but whatever I do she never seems to be happy.

24

COUNSELLOR RESPONSE: It seems as though you just can't please your girlfriend.

Example 3
CLIENT STATEMENT: Yesterday I rushed around, I seemed to have no time to myself, I went from one place to another and it was really hard to fit everything in.
COUNSELLOR RESPONSE: You had a very full day yesterday.

Do you understand what is meant by "paraphrasing" or "reflection of content" now? What the counsellor does is literally to tell the client, in a clear brief way, in the counsellor's own words, the most important things that the client has just told the counsellor. The counsellor tries to capture the essential ingredients of what the client is saying and reflect these back. This method alone, together with minimal responses, can be used successfully throughout a complete counselling session, if it is carried out by a skilful person who is capable of accurately and clearly reflecting content.

The following transcript of a short counselling session between myself as the client and an experienced counsellor, Margaret Hegarty, effectively demonstrates the way in which paraphrasing alone can be used to bring a client to a sense of resolution.

Transcript of a counselling session using paraphrasing

DAVID: Hello Margaret.
MARGARET: Hi Dave.
DAVID: Margaret, I'd like to talk to you, um, about some stuff that's really troubling me at the moment.
MARGARET: Um-hm.
DAVID: I'm getting very uptight and worrying a lot about things and I thought that perhaps having a chat with you would help.
MARGARET: Mm-hm, you're feeling anxious Dave and you'd like to talk about the things that are worrying you.
DAVID: Yes I would. Umm. What's getting me down is ah, really that I feel totally overloaded and I feel as though I'm just not coping with the amount that I've got to do and that there is just too much going on in my life.
MARGARET: Umm mm. Lots of pressure in relation to what's happening to you in your life at the moment.
DAVID: Yes. All the parts of my life seem to be pushing in on top of each other and it seems like the week just isn't long enough. There's my work, there's, umm, training that I'm doing outside my work and there's also trying to maintain social contacts and social relationships, and there just isn't time to fit them in.

MARGARET: Mm-hm.

DAVID: I feel as though I'm going under.

MARGARET: Mm-hm. You feel overcrowded with work, other pressures outside work and not enough time for your social life, and it's really getting you down.

DAVID: Yes it is getting me down, and I'm starting to despair about it. I just don't know how to get over the problem, I feel sort of trapped and the more I struggle, the more the work seems to build up and the worse the situation seems to get. I really don't know whether I'll ever be able to get myself out of this.

MARGARET: Right now it seems like, Dave, you can't see a way out, you're really hooked in there.

DAVID: No I can't. Umm, I suppose the part of my life that is most crowded is my work, and it seems like that's expanding to push out the other parts of my life, so that there's more and more work coming my way, my working hours are getting longer, they're getting more crowded and I'm starting to feel, "Oh dear, I wish I could take a break".

MARGARET: OK, so work is the main pressure in your life, it's taking over and becoming a really heavy load by the sound of things.

DAVID: Yes it is, and I guess it's a bit of a trap because I'm a counsellor and as a result of being a counsellor, I find that people who are emotionally disturbed make demands on me. They think that I'm available at any time and it's very hard for me to say, "No I won't see you because I haven't an appointment space for a couple of weeks". It's umm, it's much easier for me to say, "Oh well I'll fit you in my lunch break or I'll work back late tonight, or I'll come in early in the morning," and umm, as a result I'm caught up in feeling that there's no way that I can reduce the amount of work I've got to do.

MARGARET: What seems to be happening at work is that you find it very difficult to say "No" when you see people who need your help and consequently your lunch breaks and after hours are becoming overloaded with taking on and meeting those people's needs.

DAVID: Yes, that's right and I suppose that's the essence of my problem—that I haven't yet learnt how to say "No" properly and I haven't yet learnt how to set limits on what I do, and I guess that talking to you now, I'm starting to realize that maybe it's time that I did start to say, "No, I've got needs, I can't always be looking after other people's needs first".

MARGARET: Dave you seem to be saying that the answer is to learn to say "No" and set some limits, but that will be difficult for you in that you haven't been able to do that up to now.

DAVID: Yes, you're right! I now realize that the problem lies within me, and

I'm sure I can attend to the issue and learn to say "No". Thank you for listening to me.

If you look through the transcript above, you will notice that Margaret has used no other responses except minimal responses and reflection of content. Sometimes she combined a minimal response with paraphrasing as she started some responses by saying "Mm-hm", which really was an acknowledgement that she had heard what I said. She then continued by paraphrasing what I had told her. Did you notice as you read the transcript that there was a natural flow in the conversation? Each time I made a statement as the client, and Margaret paraphrased it, her reflection of my statement set off a train of thoughts for me so that I continued with the conversation in a natural way. Consequently, it seemed to me at the time that Margaret really was understanding what I was saying. She wasn't intruding on my thoughts in any way by putting her own ideas in on top of what I was thinking. Consequently I was able to follow my own train of thought. Each time I made a statement, by reflecting back what I said, Margaret was able to help me think clearly about what I had said and this enabled me to continue talking about the same issue, in a constructive way. It was as though I was walking along a path, in my thoughts, with Margaret walking alongside me. That was a good feeling. At times I was just buried in my thoughts, rather than concentrating on Margaret being there. It was easy to do that because Margaret's paraphrasing didn't intrude, it didn't take my mind away from the real issues that I was trying to resolve. If she had used a different style of response, her responses could quite easily have distracted me from the process of following my own train of thoughts. You will notice that even though the encounter was short, I came to a firm conclusion for me, so in fact I resolved my issue without Margaret asking questions, without Margaret putting in suggestions, and without Margaret giving advice. All she did was just to reflect back to me what I was saying.

It's important for you to learn how to paraphrase. In order to help you to do this I have provided some more examples of paraphrasing below. In each case cover up the counsellor response with a sheet of paper, read the client statement and see whether you can produce a suitable counsellor response to the client's statement.

Further examples of paraphrasing

Example 1
CLIENT STATEMENT: Within a week I've had a rates notice, an electricity bill, my car broke down and I've had to spend $200 having it fixed, there was a big

dinner that I had to attend as part of my work and it was very expensive, and in addition I've had to fork out money for my son's trip overseas and for my daughter's school fees.

COUNSELLOR RESPONSE: You've had a lot of expenses to meet in a very short time.

Example 2

CLIENT STATEMENT: Now that my father has died I can't help thinking about him. I think about the good times I had with him when I was young and about the way he showed so much interest in me in the early days of my marriage. I remember the way in which he played with my children, his grandchildren. He always seemed to be enjoying himself.

COUNSELLOR RESPONSE: You have some good memories of your father.

Example 3

CLIENT STATEMENT: The house is old and ramshackle, the rooms are very large, there isn't much in it and it needs redecorating. Parts of it are starting to fall down. Where you walk there are bare floorboards and they creak. It doesn't sound very much like home because it is such a big, open, old, barren sort of a place, but you know I really like living there.

COUNSELLOR RESPONSE: Even though the house is in poor condition it's home to you.

Example 4

CLIENT STATEMENT: I used to have a very bad drinking problem so I stopped drinking for a couple of years. Well last night I had a drink and now I'm just wondering how that's going to affect me in the future. I'm really surprised though because I was able to have just one drink and stop, whereas in the past I always used to carry on drinking once I'd started.

COUNSELLOR RESPONSE: Although you surprised yourself, you're not too sure how you'll cope with alcohol from now on.

Example 5

CLIENT STATEMENT: My daughter's a very attractive girl, she's good looking and vivacious, she dresses very nicely and she is a good natured person. She often smiles and seems to be very happy.

COUNSELLOR RESPONSE: Your daughter has many positive qualities.

Please remember that no two counsellors will use the same paraphrase. No two counsellors will pick up on the same detail, and I really do not believe that there is always one best response. The model answers that I have given above are not necessarily the best. I believe that I am a good counsellor, but I do not consider myself to be perfect in any of the micro-skills. I have yet to find someone who is. It's really important to remember that it doesn't matter how perfect your responses are. What does matter is that you create a real, trusting, caring, empathic relationship in which you are genuinely yourself. This may mean sometimes being a bungler, and occasionally saying something inappropriate. I have many times given an inappropriate response. Although I try not to do that, there will always be times when I do. I used to think that it was a disaster to give an inappropriate response until an artist friend of mine talked to me about pencil sketching. I told her how it was that when I tried to sketch I very often had the sketch three-quarters complete and then ruined it by putting in a dark line in an inappropriate place. My artist friend laughed and said, "You never draw lines in the wrong place, because whenever you put in a line you can use it to create something different". I learnt a lesson from what she said and applied it to my counselling. When I make an inappropriate response, I use that response. It will generate an interaction between myself and the client, and I am able to encourage the client to explore the effect that the inappropriate response had on her. By doing this I am using the immediacy of the relationship between myself and the client. Immediacy will be discussed more fully in Chapter 18.

In this chapter you have learnt about paraphrasing or reflection of content. Paraphrasing is really a very simple skill to use because all you have to do is to listen and to repeat back in your own words the essence of what the client has said. By doing this the client feels that you have heard her and also becomes more fully aware of what she has said. She is then able to really savour the importance of what she herself is talking about and to sort out her confusion. Remember that paraphrasing is not the same as parroting. Parroting involves repeating word for word what the client has said to you. Occasionally it may be useful to parrot the client's last few words, to enable her to continue a half-finished statement, but as a general rule, paraphrasing is a much more helpful process. This is because paraphrasing picks out the most important and salient parts of the content rather than just repeating the words the client has used. Continually repeating part or all of what the client has said would be likely to annoy the client rather then create a good relationship. Skilful reflection of content in the counsellor's own words does the reverse. It makes the client feel valued, listened to, and heard, and is useful in helping the client to move forward in her exploration.

6 Reflection of feelings

As explained in the previous chapter, one of the best ways to help a client to feel that you are listening to him is to reflect back to him the content of what he is saying. You might have noticed that in the transcript of a counselling session which was included in the previous chapter the counsellor's reflection of content included reference to feelings which the client had mentioned. For example, Margaret's third response as a counsellor included the words "you're feeling anxious Dave". This reflection was very useful for me, David, the client, because it enabled me to fully experience my anxiety rather than to push it to one side. Instead of avoiding that anxiety I was encouraged to accept its painfulness and consequently to continue to explore it more fully. The consequence of this was that the anxiety dissipated.

Reflection of feelings is one of the most important micro-skills. It is at the same time similar to and different from paraphrasing. It is similar because it involves reflecting back to the client information provided by the client. However it is different because it deals with emotional feelings, whereas paraphrasing generally deals with the information and thoughts which make up the content of what the client is saying.

Feelings are quite different from thoughts. Thoughts mill around in our brains. They are at a head level, whereas feelings are to do with emotions. Feelings are at a gut level not a head level, and they tie into our physiological sensations. For example, a person who is feeling tense emotionally may experience the tension in his muscles, often in the neck or shoulders, and an anxious person may have sweaty palms, an increased heart-rate or the sensation of "butterflies in the stomach". Frequently clients try to avoid exploring their feelings because they want to avoid the pain associated with strong emotions such as sadness, despair, anger, and anxiety. I know that for me personally, it's much less painful to philosophize about my problems, and to discuss them as though they were "out there" and didn't really belong to me. Unfortunately when I avoid my feelings, philosophize, and talk in a general way about my problems rather than fully experiencing the effect which they have on me emotionally, I rarely feel better or reach a resolution. Instead, I tend to go around in circles and get nowhere. However, if I get in touch with my feelings, own them, and experience them fully, then I usually move forward, to feel better emotionally and maybe then to make sensible

31

decisions for myself. There is consequently a conflict for many new counsellors.

In our culture we learn from childhood to comfort people by encouraging them to run away from their feelings. We are taught to say "Don't cry, it'll be all right", when it quite probably won't be all right, and the person really needs to cry to release his emotional pain. If you are to be an effective counsellor you will need to unlearn what you learnt as a child. You will need to encourage your clients to experience their emotions, to be sad, to cry, to be angry and to shout, to be overwhelmed, to be amused, to be frightened or whatever. By doing this you will help them to gain from emotional release and to move forward. This healing process of emotional release is called catharsis.

New counsellors often have problems in distinguishing between thoughts and feelings because people often use the word "feel" when they are describing a thought. For example if I say "I feel angry" then I am expressing a feeling, but if I say "I feel that counsellors learn best through practical experience" I am really not expressing a feeling at all but rather a thought and I would have been more accurate if I'd said "I think that counsellors learn best through practical experience". The words "feel that" followed by a string of words generally mean that a thought is being expressed and not a feeling. Feelings are usually expressed by one word. For example I can feel "angry", "sad", "depressed", "frustrated", "miserable", "tense", "relaxed", "happy" or "frantic". Each of these feelings is expressed by one word, whereas thoughts can only be expressed by using a string of words.

When a counsellor reflects back a feeling to a client he does not necessarily need to use the word "feel" at all. Here are some options for reflecting feelings:

"You're feeling angry" or "You feel angry" or "You're angry"
"You're feeling happy" or "You feel happy" or "You're happy".

An experienced counsellor continually identifies his client's feelings and reflects them back at the appropriate times. Sometimes a client will tell you directly how he is feeling and at other times you will be able to assess what he is feeling by listening to the content of what he is saying or by noting non-verbal behaviour or by listening to the tone of his voice.

With practice it is easy to identify feelings such as tension, distress and sadness from a person's body-posture, facial expressions and movements. Tears starting to well up in your client's eyes might let you know about his sadness. Sometimes people need permission to cry because in our culture crying, particularly by men, is often considered to be unacceptable. I sometimes say to a client "I can see the tears in your eyes" or "For me, it's OK if you cry" or just "It's OK to cry" in a gentle accepting tone of voice, and then the tears will start to flow. Allow your client to cry. Don't hand him tissues or comfort him in any way until the emotion subsides naturally. If you intrude on the crying process then the client will withdraw from his feelings, will not experience them fully, and the healing effects of emotional release will be diminished.

Be prepared for a possible dramatic response from your client whenever you reflect feelings. For a new counsellor this is sometimes alarming, but it is always useful for the client. If you correctly say to your client "I get the impression that you are really hurting inside", then the client will get in touch with his hurt feelings and may start to cry, and you will need to deal with the feelings generated in you by his crying.

Sometimes, when you reflect back anger by saying "You're angry" or perhaps "You sound very angry" the client will respond by angrily snapping back with "I'm not angry" followed by an angry tirade, often directed at the counsellor. If this happens, allow yourself to feel good, because you have enabled the client to express anger which he does not wish to own openly. He has been able to discharge some of his anger onto you, and he will feel better for that. Dealing with angry clients does occasionally have its dangers and so a full chapter has been devoted to this topic (Chapter 20).

Human beings can be likened to the old-fashioned pressure cooker. When we are functioning effectively we have sufficient emotional energy inside us to keep us motivated to live our daily lives functionally and creatively. At crisis times in our lives the emotional pressure builds up until we are ready to explode. In this state our thought processes are blocked and we are unable to cope. We feel out of control of ourselves. To regain control we first need to release some of the emotional pressure, and this is difficult as most of us have been taught from childhood to hold our emotions in, not to cry, and not to be angry. An effective counsellor enables the client to fully experience his emotions and to feel better as a result of cathartic release. With cathartic release the pressure in the pressure cooker goes back to normal and rational thinking can start to take place again, so that constructive decision making can occur. Reflection of feelings is therefore, as stated previously, one of the most important, perhaps *the* most important counselling skill.

Here are some examples of client statements, followed by suitable reflections of feeling. Before reading the counsellor response in each case, write down the response that you would give.

Examples of reflection of feelings

Example 1

CLIENT STATEMENT: I keep expecting my mother to show more interest in me. Time and again I've asked her to come over to see me but she never does. Yesterday it was my birthday and she did come to visit me, but do you know she didn't even remember that it was my birthday. I just don't think she cares about me at all. (Said slowly in a flat tone of voice.)

COUNSELLOR RESPONSE: "You're disappointed" or "You feel hurt".

Example 2

CLIENT STATEMENT: First of all, my brother broke my electric drill. He didn't bother to tell me that he'd broken it, he just left it lying. Then what do you think he did, he went and borrowed my motorbike without telling me. I feel like thumping him.

COUNSELLOR RESPONSE: "You're very angry" or "You're furious".

Example 3

CLIENT STATEMENT: I got a new job recently. It's quite different from the old one. The boss is nice to me, I've got a good office to work in, the whole atmosphere in the firm is really positive. I can't believe that I'm so lucky.

COUNSELLOR RESPONSE: "You feel really happy" or "You're really happy".

Example 4

CLIENT STATEMENT: Young people nowadays aren't like they used to be in my day, dressed smartly; they're dirty, they're rude, they don't stand for you in buses, I don't know what's become of the new generation!

COUNSELLOR RESPONSE: "You're disgusted".

Example 5

CLIENT STATEMENT: My boyfriend just rang me from his hotel overseas. He's a reporter and is in a real trouble spot. While I was talking to him on the phone I could hear angry voices in the background, and then there was an incredible crash, and the line went dead, and I don't know what's happened to him! (Said very quickly and breathlessly.)

COUNSELLOR RESPONSE: "You're terribly worried" or "You're panicking".

These examples probably gave you an idea of how difficult it is to assess the feelings underlying a client statement when non-verbal cues including facial expression and body posture are not available. When you are actively engaged in a counselling interaction with a client it will be easier for you to identify what the client is feeling because you will have the use of all your senses. If you are attending closely to your client your own feelings will start to match his. When he is hurting, at a less intense level, you will experience something of his hurt and will be able to reflect it back to him.

With experience at reflecting feelings you will be able to use a variety of expressions so that your responses sound natural rather than stereotyped and somewhat mechanical. Sometimes a short response such as "You're hurting" is appropriate. But at other times you might use expressions such as the following:

"I get the impression that you are really hurting now."
"From what you are saying my guess is that you are hurting deep down."
"Right now you're hurting."

As a general rule try to keep your counselling responses short. Remember that it is desirable for the client to do most of the talking and that your job is to listen and hear. Long counsellor responses intrude on the client's own inner processes and prevent the client from freely and openly exploring his issues.

When you have fully mastered reflection of feelings move ahead to the next chapter and learn to combine reflection of content with reflection of feelings.

7 Reflection of content and feeling

Hopefully by now you will have mastered the skills needed to comfortably use minimal responses, reflection of content and reflection of feelings. These three types of response are the most basic and important ones, because together they provide a foundation onto which other skills can be added. With experience you will find that you can quite often combine reflection of content with reflection of feelings. For example, the statement "You feel disappointed because your brother didn't do as he promised" is a statement which includes both feeling and content. The feeling is one of disappointment, the content is to do with the reasons for being disappointed, that is, because the brother didn't do as he promised. So that the idea of combining reflection of feeling and content becomes clearer, let us look at a few examples. Firstly, we will take another look at the examples given in Chapter 6, but this time the counsellor responses will include reflection of both feeling and content, whereas in Chapter 6, reflection of feeling alone was used. Notice that the responses are short and not wordy.

Examples of reflection of feeling and content

Example 1
CLIENT STATEMENT: I keep expecting my mother to show more interest in me. Time and again I've asked her to come over to see me but she never does. Yesterday it was my birthday and she did come to visit me, but do you know she didn't even remember that it was my birthday. I just don't think she cares about me at all. (Said slowly in a flat tone of voice.)
COUNSELLOR RESPONSE: "You're disappointed by your mother's behaviour" or "You feel hurt by your mother's apparent lack of caring".

Example 2
CLIENT STATEMENT: First of all, my brother broke my electric drill. He didn't bother to tell me that he'd broken it, he just left it lying there. Then what do you think he did, he went and borrowed my motorbike without telling me. I feel like thumping him.
COUNSELLOR RESPONSE: "You're very angry with your brother" or "You're furious with your brother".

37

Example 3

CLIENT STATEMENT: I got a new job recently. It's quite different from the old one. The boss is nice to me, I've got a good office to work in, the whole atmosphere in the firm is really positive. I can't believe that I'm so lucky.

COUNSELLOR RESPONSE: "You feel really happy with your new job" or "You're really happy with your new job".

Example 4

CLIENT STATEMENT: Young people nowadays aren't like they used to be in my day, dressed smartly; they're dirty, they're rude, they don't stand for you in buses, I don't know what's become of the new generation!

COUNSELLOR RESPONSE: "Young people disgust you" or "You feel disgusted by the younger generation's behaviour".

Example 5

CLIENT STATEMENT: My boyfriend just rang me from his hotel overseas. He's a reporter and is in a real trouble spot. While I was talking to him on the phone I could hear angry voices in the background, and then there was an incredible crash, and the line went dead, and I don't know what's happened to him! (Said very quickly and breathlessly.)

COUNSELLOR RESPONSE: "You sound really worried about what might have happened to your boyfriend".

Further examples of reflection of feeling and content

Here are some more client statements for you to practise with. In each case, invent a suitable counsellor response and write it down. Then compare your response with the one supplied at the end of this chapter.

Example 1

CLIENT STATEMENT: I'm getting very worn out, whenever anything goes wrong I get blamed. I spend my time running around looking after other people's needs and in return I get no thanks and lots of criticism. It's just not fair. The more I do the less I'm appreciated.

Example 2

CLIENT STATEMENT: You just wouldn't believe the dishwasher has broken down, the washing machine still hasn't been fixed, my husband ran the car into a post, my daughter's bike has a puncture, I just can't believe it, so much is going wrong. What's going to go wrong next? I just can't take any more.

Example 3

CLIENT STATEMENT: I just can't understand my son and daughter. They always want to be together, but whenever they are together they fight. It doesn't seem to matter what I suggest they do when they're together, they start an argument. It's incessant, it never stops and now I'm starting to get like them, I'm starting to get angry and irritable too. Sometimes I'm so angry that I could knock their heads together.

Example 4

CLIENT STATEMENT: I've done everything I can to get her back. I've given her presents, I've phoned her, I've written her letters, sent messages through her friends, I've said I'm sorry, and I've even offered to go and get counselling with her, but whatever I do I just can't get through to her and she just won't come back to me. I just can't live without her!

Example 5

CLIENT STATEMENT: I can't understand why my landlord won't give me my bond back but he won't. I cleaned the flat, I left it in good condition, I know he doesn't like me and he just won't give me the bond back. I know I really ought to go and confront him and say to him that this isn't fair. It's not fair. I even got my friends to come round and help me clean up. I spent two days trying to made the place decent, and it was beautiful when I walked out, but he still won't give me the money back. I really ought to go and confront him, but he's a big man and he tends to be very angry at times and you never know—if there was an argument he might hit me!

Example 6

CLIENT STATEMENT: I went next door to ask my neighbour if he would drive me over to my boyfriend's place because I'm worried about him. I know it's a long way, but I'm sure my neighbour could do it. All he said was, "No, I can't afford the petrol, and in any case I don't want to go out in this bad weather". I can't understand how he can be so callous because my boyfriend could be seriously ill for all I know. I just can't understand how my neighbour can sit and do nothing, and I'm sure that if it was one of his friends, someone he cared about, that he would go out tonight.

As stated previously, it's desirable for a counsellor to keep his responses short so as not to intrude on the client's inner processes. Long statements will take the client away from what he is experiencing and will bring him out of his own world and into the counsellor's world. You have just been learning how to combine the skills of reflection of content and reflection of feelings, and there are times when it is appropriate to use this combined type of response.

However, at other times it will be more appropriate, in the interests of brevity, to use either reflection of content, or reflection of feeling, but not both. This is particularly true when using reflection of feeling. Sometimes reflecting the feeling alone, without mention of content, can be more powerful in helping the client to own a feeling which he may be trying to suppress. If a counsellor says "You're really hurting" the statement focuses on the client's pain rather than encouraging the client to escape from experiencing his pain by latching onto "content" words and moving into a cognitive rather than feeling level of experiencing. Whenever possible, help clients to experience their emotional feelings rather than to suppress feelings by working at a head or cognitive level. Experiencing feelings fully is often painful, but is cathartic and consequently therapeutically desirable.

You have now learnt how to use the three basic skills. That is, the skills of, "minimal responding", "reflection of content" and "reflection of feelings". It is essential that these three skills should be practised until they are fully mastered before you proceed with learning any of the other micro-skills. Initially, during the learning process, you are likely to feel awkward in using these skills and this awkwardness may get transmitted to the client. Keep practising until you can use the skills in a natural way which does not seem to be contrived or artificial. Once this has been achieved, the counselling interaction will flow smoothly and you will not feel pressured to think of "smart" responses. Instead your listening skills will be enhanced and you will feel more relaxed and spontaneous. Interestingly, if the skills are used competently, the client will not realize that you are primarily using reflection, but will feel as though you are listening and commenting in a sensible way on what is being said. An experienced counsellor is likely to use the three basic skills which you have now learnt more frequently than any other skills, because they enable the client to explore his world fully in his own way without interference by the counsellor, but with the certain knowledge that the counsellor is actively listening to him.

Remember that counselling is about walking alongside a person as he explores his world. Some people say that a counsellor should, metaphorically speaking, walk in the shoes of the other person. Certainly it is important that the counsellor attempts to see the world in the way the client sees the world. Thus at times, an experienced counsellor will almost get into the client's shoes, so that he can better understand what it feels like to be the client, and how it must be to look at the world from the client's viewpoint. By doing this a trusting relationship is developed which enables the client to risk exploring the most painful issues of his life, and so to move forward out of his confusion.

Suggested counsellor responses for further examples on reflection of feeling and content

EXAMPLE 1: "You feel resentful because other people don't appreciate your efforts."

EXAMPLE 2: "So many things have gone wrong that you're starting to feel pressured and unable to cope" or "You just can't cope with everything going wrong."

EXAMPLE 3: "The continual fighting between your son and daughter infuriates you."

EXAMPLE 4: "You feel desperate because you can't get your wife to come back to you."

EXAMPLE 5: "Even though you believe the landlord is being unfair you're too scared to confront him."

EXAMPLE 6: "You're disgusted by your neighbour's unwillingness to help."

8 The seeing, hearing, and feeling modes

You are unique because you are a human being. I am unique, I am a human being. Being unique is important to me, I'm not quite the same as you, and you're not quite the same as me. All of us in the world are a bit different from each other. The ways in which we do things are different, and most importantly, the ways in which we experience and think about the world are different. An important difference in the way individuals experience the world has to do with the senses that we all use for maintaining contact with our environment. As you are well aware, there are a number of different senses that we use to experience our world. We can smell, taste, touch, see, and hear. Smelling, tasting and touching are bodily sensations due to external stimuli, which together with our internal physical sensations link up with our emotional feelings. These sensations and feelings combine to contribute to our awareness of the world. Together, they make up what is generally referred to as the *kinaesthetic or feeling* mode of awareness. Similarly, we may be aware of our world by using either the seeing mode or the hearing mode of awareness. Hence we can describe three different ways in which we can experience the world through our senses, and these are the *kinaesthetic or feeling mode*, the *seeing or visual mode*, and the *hearing or auditory mode*.

We all have different abilities. Some of us are good at maths, others at languages, and some are good at doing things with their hands. During our lives most of us discover those things that we do well and those things that we are not so good at. In the same way that we develop different practical and academic abilities during our lives, some of us learn to use particular senses more effectively than other senses. For example, there are people who are very good at detecting things that smell, and other people who have acute hearing and can hear the slightest sound. Some people are really observant and readily notice small details which others miss. When I learnt to be a scuba diver, the fellow who taught me was extremely observant and would frequently see things that I missed. He would see the heavily camouflaged and dangerous stone fish lurking among the rocks where I was probing, whereas I would fail to see it until it was pointed out to me.

Not only do people experience the world differently, but as explained by Bandler and Grinder, the pioneers of Neuro Linguistic Programming, people think in different ways. Some people think predominantly by using

42

visual imagery (the seeing mode), others think in the hearing mode by talking to themselves mentally, and others think in terms of their feelings and bodily sensations (kinaesthetic or feeling mode). There may be people who are equally versatile and can think easily in all or any of the three modes, but most people seem to rely more strongly on one mode than the others. What mode do you think in? Are you predominantly visual, auditory, or kinaesthetic.

If you listen to someone talking, and you listen carefully to words being used, you are likely to get some clues as to which mode he generally uses when he is thinking. Let me give you a few examples. Some people use expressions like "I hear what you say", "It sounds like you mean", "It sounds as though", "Tell me what happened", or "That rings bells for me". People who use that sort of language are using the hearing mode of thinking. There are other people of course who will say things like, "I see what you mean", "I've got a clearer picture of the situation", or "It looks good". People who talk like that are using the seeing mode to think. The third category of people are people who predominately think and experience the world by using kinaesthetic methods. They say things like "It feels good", "You touched a raw nerve there" or "I sense your discomfort".

Previously we've considered the value of matching the way in which the client behaves. We've talked about how it's helpful to sit in a similar way to the client, to talk at the same pace and with the same tone of voice as the client, and to match the client's breathing. Doing these things gives the client a feeling of togetherness with the counsellor, so that the client feels comfortable, safe and able to share openly. Another way in which a counsellor can join with a client is by using similar language to the client's. If a client is using predominately "seeing" language, then you will need to use "seeing" language too, if you are to properly connect with him. Similarly, if a client is using "hearing" language, in order to join with that client properly, you will need to use hearing language yourself and of course the same is true when it comes to "kinaesthetic" or "feeling" language. It's really quite fun to try to learn the skill of matching the client's mode. When you are listening to people in general conversation, listen carefully to find out their preferred mode, and respond in the same mode. If you do this you are likely to improve your rapport with them.

There is an enjoyable way of learning to recognize the type of language being used. If you wish you can use a practice session to play a game of "spot the mode". The game goes like this; one student, or player, talks about a problem, but continually changes the type of language that he is using, flipping from "hearing" to "seeing" and to "feeling" language in random sequence. While this is happening, other students hold up one of three cards on each of which is written "hearing" or "seeing" or "feeling". If the listening

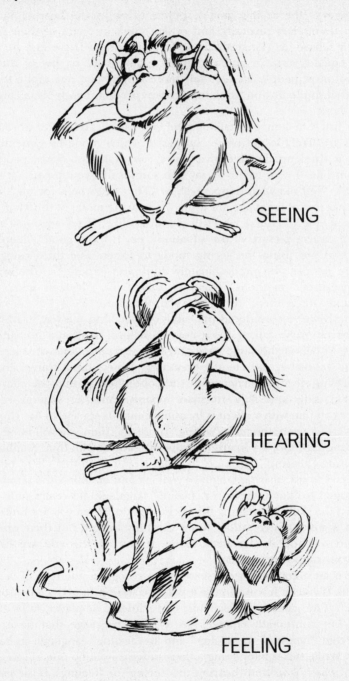

SEEING

HEARING

FEELING

students are correctly following the one who is talking, then they will all hold up a "seeing" card whenever the speaker is using "seeing" language, and similarly they will hold up a "hearing" or a "feeling" card, at appropriate times, in order to match the language being used. For your practice now, here is a paragraph in which the mode continually changes. See if you can spot when the language changes from one mode to another.

Practice example of mode changes

"I remember the scene as I sat on the sand, which was cold and wet. As I sat there, I heard some seagulls squawking as they flew overhead casting shadows on the sand, and I could hear the waves crashing. On the horizon, I noticed a ship steaming along, and at the same time a young man's footsteps thumped past me as he ran along the beach. I thought about what was going to happen later in the day and could picture the beautiful house which we were going to visit for tea. I imagined myself walking through the garden of the house and admiring the beautiful flowers that grew there. My body tingled with excitement in anticipation, and I told myself to be patient."

I wonder how many changes of mode you found in the above paragraph. According to my count there were nine. See the end of this chapter to find out how I arrived at this figure.

Practice examples of counsellor responses

The following are some examples of client statements and counsellor responses. In each case, notice that the response is in the correct mode, that is, either the hearing, feeling or seeing mode. Once again it is suggested that you cover up the given response and invent a response yourself. You can then compare your response with the one provided.

Example 1
CLIENT STATEMENT: I went back there once more, but as before, the place gave me bad vibes. I had to leave because my stomach was churning and my hands were sweating.
COUNSELLOR RESPONSE: You felt so uncomfortable that you left. (Kinaesthetic mode.)

Example 2
CLIENT STATEMENT: In the past, my mother has frequently criticized my wife, and I have always listened to what she has said. Recently though, I've started

to question what she's told me and I'm inclined to say that some of her statements about Monica may be wrong.

COUNSELLOR RESPONSE: It sounds as though you've got doubts about the accuracy of what your mother tells you. (Hearing mode.)

Example 3

CLIENT STATEMENT: She gave me a bunch of flowers and I was really touched by that. In fact, I feel quite different about our relationship now because the coldness we experienced before has been replaced by warmth.

COUNSELLOR RESPONSE: Your feelings towards her have changed, and are now very pleasant. (Kinaesthetic mode.)

Example 4

CLIENT STATEMENT: It seems to me that the writing's on the wall, there's nothing that I can do to save the situation, and I can see nothing but disaster from now on.

COUNSELLOR RESPONSE: The outlook's a really bad one. (Seeing mode.)

Example 5

CLIENT STATEMENT: It's as though there is a brick wall around him. It has no door, and no way in or out. When I look over the wall I see a very strange person.

COUNSELLOR RESPONSE: You picture him as a strange man surrounded by a brick wall. (Seeing mode.)

Example 6

CLIENT STATEMENT: When she spoke it was as though a bell was ringing in my head warning me not to prejudge what she was saying. Consequently I heard what she told me, responded sensibly, and then said to myself "Well done, you've avoided another terrible argument."

COUNSELLOR RESPONSE: You listened to your own internal warning system and the outcome sounds good. (Hearing mode.)

In your practice sessions, continue to practise those skills that you have already learnt; that is, minimal responses, and reflection of content and feelings. In addition, practise matching the client's language by using the same mode. If you do this, then the words you use will be more meaningful for him. Note that the ideas expressed in this chapter have their origins in Neuro Linguistic Programming. If these ideas strongly appeal to you then you may wish to study Neuro Linguistic Programming in depth once you have mastered basic counselling skills (see the suggestions below for further reading).

Modes used in practice example

I remember the scene as I sat on the sand	Seeing
which was cold and wet. As I sat there	Feeling (first change)
I heard some seagulls squawking as they	Hearing (second change)
flew overhead casting shadows on the sand,	Seeing (third change)
and I could hear the waves crashing.	Hearing (fourth change)
On the horizon I noticed a ship steaming along	Seeing (fifth change)
and at the same time a young man's footsteps thumped past me as he ran along the beach.	Hearing (sixth change)
I thought about what was going to happen later in the day and could picture the beautiful house which we were going to visit for tea. I imagined myself walking through the garden of the house and admiring the beautiful flowers that grew there.	Seeing (seventh change)
My body tingled with excitement in anticipation	Feeling (eighth change)
and I told myself to be patient.	Hearing (ninth change)

Further reading on Neuro Linguistic Programming

Bandler, R. and Grinder, J. *Frogs into Princes: Neuro-Linguistic Programming.* Moab: Real People Press, 1979.

Lankton, S. R. *Practical Majic—A Translation of Basic Neuro-Linguistic Programming into Clinical Psychotherapy.* Cupertino: Meta, 1980.

Lewis, B. A. and Pucelik, R. F. *Majic Demystified—A Pragmatic Guide to Communication Change.* Oregon: Metamorphous, 1982

9 Asking questions

You may be surprised that a chapter on asking questions should come so late in this book, after you have already learnt several other skills. Well, surprisingly, it's not necessary to ask questions very often at all in most counselling interviews. Certainly this is true for interviews which are concerned with counselling people for emotional problems. Most of the information that the counsellor needs to know will emerge naturally without asking questions if the counsellor actively listens to the client, uses the skills which have already been learnt, and skilfully reflects back the content and feeling of what the client is saying.

It's very tempting for new counsellors to ask lots of questions. If you find yourself repeatedly asking questions, it's important for you to ask yourself what your goal is in asking these questions. If your goal is to stimulate the client into talking, then you may well be using the wrong approach. More often than not, simply reflecting back what has already been said will stimulate the client into further confidence sharing without the need for you to ask a question. If a counsellor asks too many questions the counselling session becomes more like an interrogation and the client is likely to be less open and less communicative. The counsellor then ends up controlling the direction in which the interview will go. This is, as a general rule, unfortunate, because it is desirable for the client to go in whatever direction her energy leads her. It's important for the client to fully explore the area in which her problem lies. Often a client won't zero in on her real problem until she has spent some time wandering around the general problem area. If the counsellor tries to find out what is really troubling her by asking questions the client may never move towards the most painful things that are causing trouble, but may in fact just go off at a tangent in a direction of the counsellor's choosing. Another problem with excessive question-asking is that the client will quickly learn to expect questions, and may wait for the counsellor to ask another question instead of thinking out for herself what is important. There is therefore a real danger in asking unnecessary questions and it is my view that question asking should be limited to those situations in which there is little alternative but to ask a question. When you do ask a question be clear about what it is that you hope to achieve by asking the question. Before looking at the goals which can be achieved through asking questions we need to think about the types of question we can ask.

There are two major categories into which questions fall. Some questions are called "open questions" and other questions are called "closed questions". Both types of question can be useful in the counselling process and it is necessary for you to fully understand the difference between the two types. Then it will become clear to you when it is appropriate to use which type.

Closed questions are questions that lead to a specific answer. Usually the answer to a closed question is very short. It may be an answer like "Yes" or "No". Consider for example the closed question. "Did you come here by bus today?" Obviously the most probable answer is either "Yes" or "No". The client may choose to expand on the answer but is unlikely to do so. Closed questions such as "Do you love your wife?" and "Are you angry?" usually lead to the answer "Yes" or "No". If I ask the closed question "How many years have you lived in California?" the answer might be "twenty-four", and it is a specific answer. There are times in a counselling session when you will need to ask closed questions because you require a specific answer to a very definite question. There are also other important reasons for asking closed questions as we shall see later. However, there is a problem with asking closed questions and I think that it will probably be apparent to you already. If you ask a closed question, it is possible that the client may continue to talk to you and to enlarge on the answer she has given, but it is not necessary for the client to do that. Moreover, you have limited the client in the sense that the sort of answer that she can give, if she answers your question, is very restricted. A lawyer in a courtroom likes to ask closed questions so that the client is restricted in the range of answers that can be given. Counsellors are not lawyers and generally the counsellor's intention is to free the client up so that she can speak more openly.

The open question is very different in its effect from the closed question. It gives the client lots of scope, allows the client to explore any relevant area, and in fact encourages the client to freely divulge additional material. If I ask the closed question "Did you come here by bus?" the answer is likely to be "Yes" or "No". Contrast this with the open question "How did you travel here?". The client is freer to answer the open question by talking about the way she travelled and the answer is likely to be richer in information. Some more examples to illustrate the difference between closed and open questions are presented below. In each case read the closed question and try to replace it by an equivalent open question yourself before reading the suggested alternative.

Example 1
Closed question: Do you feel angry?
Open question: How do you feel?

Example 2

CLOSED QUESTION: How many children do you have?
OPEN QUESTION: Tell me about your children?

Example 3

CLOSED QUESTION: Do you argue with your wife often?
OPEN QUESTION: What is your relationship like with your wife?

Example 4

CLOSED QUESTION: Did you punish your son when he misbehaved?
OPEN QUESTION: What did you do when your son misbehaved?

Example 5

CLOSED QUESTION: Do you love your husband?
OPEN QUESTION: Can you tell me about your feelings toward your husband?

Example 6

CLOSED QUESTION: Is the atmosphere tense at home?
OPEN QUESTION: What's the atmosphere like at home?

If you look at the closed questions above, you will realize that the client has little room for using her own imagination when giving an answer. The sort of answer that she will give to a closed question will be direct and probably short. A closed question doesn't encourage the client to be creative and share new information with the counsellor, but tends to confine the client to a limited response. The open question is quite different as you can see from the above examples. In each case, by asking an open question, the counsellor might get unexpected additional information. If you look at the open question "Tell me about your children" you will realize that the client could give a number of quite different answers. For example, the client might say "My children are beautiful and very happy" or "I have two sons and a daughter" or "My children are all grown up and my wife and I live happily together on our own". It's clear from this example that by asking an open question the counsellor may get a variety of answers and may get an answer which is quite different to the one which she might have expected. This is an advantage because counsellors aren't mind readers, and can't know what the client is thinking unless the client verbalizes her thoughts. Also, it's sensible for counsellors to use questions which will encourage the client to bring out those things which are of most interest to the client, rather than those things that are of most interest to the counsellor.

There is one particular type of question that I sometimes ask but try to avoid asking. I try to avoid asking questions that begin with "Why". When I have asked "Why" questions, I've usually found that the client tends to look for an intellectually thought-out reason in reply and does not centre on what is happening internally. "Why" questions tend to generate answers that are "out there"; that is, answers that don't seem to come from inside the client and often aren't convincing. They frequently fall into the category that I would call "excuses" or "rationalizations".

As explained previously, it is generally preferable to use open questions rather than closed questions except when helping a client to be more specific, or when specific information is required. In these latter cases closed questions may sometimes be appropriate. In order to make sense of the client's story a counsellor may need to know whether the client is married, whether she has children, and what the ages of the children are. If a counsellor needs to know this information, then it may be appropriate to ask directly by using closed questions. Below are some more examples of closed and open questions. Use them to practise framing open questions.

Practice examples

Example 1
CLOSED QUESTION: Would you like fish for dinner tonight?
OPEN QUESTION: What would you like for dinner tonight?

Example 2
CLOSED QUESTION: Do you like it when your husband praises you?
OPEN QUESTION: How do you feel when your husband praises you?

Example 3
CLOSED QUESTION: Was your mother a dominating person?
OPEN QUESTION: What was your mother like? *or* How did your mother behave in her relationships with other people?"

Example 4
CLOSED QUESTION: Did your father make you come to see me?
OPEN QUESTION: What brought you here?

Example 5
CLOSED QUESTION: Did the change disrupt your life?
OPEN QUESTION: How did the change affect your life?

There are three important goals that can be achieved through question asking. These are:

1. to encourage the client to open up and disclose more;
2. to help the client be more specific or concrete;
3. to help the counsellor reach a clearer understanding of the client's situation.

The first of these goals is to help the client to open up and disclose more. From the previous discussion it should be clear that open questions are more appropriate for doing this than closed questions.

The second goal is to help the client be more specific. Clients frequently make very general, vague statements, and this is unhelpful to both the client and the counsellor because it is impossible to think clearly about a problem if it is expressed in vague, woolly, non-specific language. The counsellor's task is to help the client to clarify her thinking. For instance if a client makes a vague statement like "That sort of thing always makes me annoyed", it may not be at all clear to either the client or the counsellor what is really meant by the words "that sort of thing". It is then appropriate for the counsellor to ask the client what she means when she says "that sort of thing". Similarly, a client might say "I just can't stand it any more." The word "it" is non-specific and to help the client to clear up the vagueness the counsellor might ask "What is it that you can't stand any more?". Similarly, consider the client statement "I'm fed up with him". This is a very general statement and may need clarification, in which case the counsellor might well respond by saying "Tell me in what ways you are fed up with him." When clients make generalizations, it is often useful for the counsellor to ask closed questions to help the client be more specific and to focus on the real issue.

The third goal, in asking questions, is similar to the second. It is to help the counsellor reach a clearer understanding of the client's situation. Sometimes a client omits important bits of information, and this makes her story difficult to understand. However, requests for information should be made with caution. As a counsellor, before you ask for information, ask yourself whether you really need it. If you didn't have the information would you still be able to help the client? If the answer to that question is "yes", then asking a question is unnecessary, and the desire to ask a question probably stems from your own needs and/or curiosity. There is absolutely no justification for a counsellor seeking information in order to satisfy her own curiosity. To do so would be to pry unnecessarily into the client's affairs. Such prying merely intrudes into the counselling process and interrupts the proper flow of the counselling interaction.

In this chapter we have looked at the usefulness of closed and open questions and have discussed the differences between the two. Now is the time for you to practise using questions. There is a risk that through practising the asking of questions, you may quickly become reliant on using

them excessively. If that were to happen it would be unfortunate because instead of the client feeling that you were travelling beside her as she explored her thoughts and feelings, she would feel more as though she were being interrogated. This would greatly diminish the quality of the counselling relationship and would inhibit the client from opening up freely. When a person is continually questioned, that person tends to withdraw rather than to open up. Remember that paraphrasing and reflection of feelings are more likely to motivate the client to talk freely than asking questions. Because of this, I suggest that when you are practising asking questions you only use one question for every three responses and that the other two responses should reflect either content or feelings. If you stick to this rule during your practice sessions, and do not use more than one question in every three responses, then your continued practice of the most important basic responses will be ensured. Consequently, when you start counselling genuine clients you will be highly skilled in reflection of feelings and content, and will only use questions when reflection is not appropriate.

10   Summarizing

Up to now the skills which we have discussed have been those which have been designed to create a good counselling relationship and to encourage the client to open up, sharing with the counsellor the issues which are causing emotional distress. If we use the analogy of the counsellor walking alongside the client on a journey, then the skills which we have described up to now encourage the client to continue exploring. As he explores, the client moves in his own direction with the counsellor beside him.

From time to time it is important for the client to stop and review the ground which has recently been traversed. This review is encouraged by using the skill of *summarizing*. Summarizing is rather like paraphrasing. When the counsellor paraphrases, what he does is to reflect back to the client whatever has been said in a single client statement. Similarly, when the counsellor summarizes, what he does he is to reflect back to the client what has been said in a number of client statements. The summary draws together the main points from the content, and may also take into account the feelings that the client has described. A summary does not involve a complete re-run of the ground covered, but rather picks out the salient points, the important things that the client has been talking about, and presents them in such a way that he can get an overview of what he himself has been discussing. By doing this, the counsellor enables the client to absorb and to ponder on what he has been sharing. Summarizing clarifies what the client has been saying and puts it into an organized format so that the client is better able to see a clear picture of his situation. Frequently when a client comes to counselling he is confused. It is as though he were walking through a forest and can see nothing clearly. He is lost in a confusing jungle of overgrowth and trees. By summarizing, the counsellor assists him to see the trees more clearly and to find a path between them. Here is a short transcript of part of a practice counselling session which illustrates the use of summarizing.

Transcript to illustrate summarizing

CLIENT: You know . . . [pause] . . . I really believe in people taking responsibility for themselves . . . [pause] . . . and so I can't really understand why it is that I do so much worrying about my brothers.

COUNSELLOR: You sound puzzled by your concern for your brothers.
(Reflection of feeling and content.)

CLIENT: Yes I am concerned. I'm not too sure what it's all about because I even seem to be worrying about them when I'm at work and yet I know that they are adults and are quite capable of looking after themselves.
COUNSELLOR: Even though you know they're adults, you still worry.
(Reflection of content and feeling.)

CLIENT: Yes I do. Incessantly. I'm always thinking the worst, you know. That maybe Bill has had an accident in that crazy car which he will insist on driving around, and I'm afraid that as far as Sidney is concerned, he's just not in very good health and I'd hate anything to happen to either of them.
COUNSELLOR: Even as you speak now you sound anxious.
(Reflection of feeling.)

CLIENT: Yes I am anxious, I'm really anxious . . . [pause]
COUNSELLOR: As you experience that anxiety can you tell me more about it?
(Open question.)

CLIENT: Yes, yes I think I can, I'm just, uh-mm, becoming aware of some very painful memories that I have of my elder sister. (Said slowly and with hesitation.)
COUNSELLOR: I get the impression that you're finding it difficult to talk about your memories.
(Reflection of feeling.)

CLIENT: Yes, it's really painful for me to remember what happened to her. I was really very fond of her and I hurt a great deal when I think about the way she finished her life. (voice quivering)
COUNSELLOR: It distresses you to think about her death. (Reflection of feeling and content.)

CLIENT: Yes it does, you see she killed herself. She took an overdose and it was too late when we found her.
COUNSELLOR: I can almost feel your sadness.
(Joining statement, bringing closeness between client and counsellor.)

CLIENT: [Sobs] . . . yeah, it was very sad for me and it still is. I just wished I could have done something to have changed the way she saw her life.
COUNSELLOR: You wish that you could have helped her.
(Reflection of feeling and content.)

CLIENT: Yes, I do. I would love to have been able to put my arms around her and to tell her that I really loved her. I couldn't have told her that her life was good because it wasn't, but I could have told her that she mattered to me.

COUNSELLOR: You'd have liked to have told her how much you cared about her.
(Reflection of content.)

CLIENT: Yes I would, and that I guess would have made me feel a lot better even if she had still killed herself. I suppose it would have been much better for me if I could have told her how I felt when she was alive and now it's too late.

COUNSELLOR: You're sad because you missed an opportunity.
(Reflection of feeling and content.)

CLIENT: Yes, I did, and I suppose I'm starting to realize something about the way I feel anxious when I think about my two brothers. You see, I would really like to be able to tell them how much I care about them, but somehow I just can't.

COUNSELLOR: You've told me how you worry about your brothers and how your sister killed herself. It seems as though you're really sad because you weren't able to tell your sister that you really cared for her when she was alive and now you'd like to be able to tell your brothers that you care about them, but somehow you can't.
(Summary.)

CLIENT: You're right. That's what my problem is. I think what I need to do is to go and talk to them, and then maybe I'll stop worrying about them.

If you look at the above transcript you will see that in summarizing, the counsellor tied together the elements of what the client had said during the previous statements. This enabled the client to put the whole package together and as a result, to get some resolution for himself. The resolution was the client's own and as such was fitting for the client. It wasn't suggested by the counsellor.

Summarizing is something that needs to be done from time to time during a counselling session so that the client is able to clarify his ideas and combine the various elements of what he is saying into an understandable form. In particular, towards the end of the counselling session it is often sensible for the counsellor to summarize the main issues that were dealt with during the session. By doing this, the counsellor ties together the thoughts, ideas and feelings that were expressed in the session, leaving the client feeling less confused and better able to deal with his life situation. This tying together enables the counsellor to move towards terminating the session as explained in Chapter 16.

11 Reframing

Have you ever noticed how two people who observe the same event, such as a game of football, will give different descriptions of what happened? We all have individual perspectives, and the way that I see things may well be different from the way in which you see things. Quite often clients have a very negative way of seeing the world. They interpret events as they see them, but often from a position of depression or of low self-esteem. The counsellor needs to listen very carefully to the client's description of the events or situation, and then try to look from the client's viewpoint and picture what the client has described. The client's picture, painted from his own perspective, will have a frame which is appropriate for the client with his own particular mood and viewpoint. Sometimes a skilful counsellor can change the way a client perceives events or situations by "reframing" the picture which the client has described. The counsellor, metaphorically speaking, puts a new frame around the picture so that the picture looks different.

The idea behind reframing is not to deny the way the client sees the world, but to present the client with an expanded view of the world. Thus, if the client wishes, he may choose to see things in a new way. It would be quite useless to say to a client "Things are not really as bad as you think; cheer up!" if the client really sees the world in a very negative way. However, it may be possible to describe what the client sees in such a way that the client has a broader vision of what has occurred and thus is able to be less negative.

Here are some examples of reframing.

Examples of reframing

Example 1
The client has explained that she seems to be unable to relax, because as soon as she turns her back her young son misbehaves and she has to chase after him and punish him. The counsellor has reflected back her feelings about this and now the client is calmer. At this point the counsellor decides to offer the client a reframe concerning the behaviour of her son.
COUNSELLOR REFRAME: I get the impression that you are really important to your son and that he wants lots of attention from you.

By making this statement, the counsellor has reframed the son's behaviour in a positive way, so that the mother can feel important and

58

needed. Maybe she will start to believe that her son is really crying out for more attention and will see his behaviour instead of being designed to annoy her, as being designed to attract her attention so that he can get more of her time. By reframing the child's behaviour in this way, there is a possibility that the mother may feel more positive towards her son and that this change in relationship could bring about a change in behaviour.

Example 2

The client has explained that he is continually getting angry with his daughter who will not study and attend to her school work but instead prefers to play around with what he describes as "layabouts". He explains how he can hardly cope with his anger and he is getting uptight and feeling very, very miserable. He blames his daughter heavily for what he sees as appalling behaviour.

COUNSELLOR REFRAME: It seems as though you care so much about your daughter, you care so much about her turning out to be the sort of person that you want her to be, that you are prepared to completely sacrifice your own needs for a relaxed and enjoyable life, and are willing to make your own life a misery by putting a great deal of energy into trying to correct her behaviour.

This reframe allows the father to feel positive about himself instead of feeling negative about the way he is continually losing his temper. He may now be able to see himself as really caring about his daughter, and also may be able to see that he is putting his daughter's needs ahead of his own. He is reminded of his need to be relaxed and enjoy his life. The reframe might take some of the tension out of the situation by removing the focus from the daughter, and putting it onto the client himself.

Example 3

The client has separated from her husband against her will. Her husband is now pushing her away and hurting her badly by refusing to even talk to her or to see her at all. The client has shared her pain and suffering and the counsellor has reflected her feelings and allowed her to explore them fully. However the counsellor now reframes the husband's behaviour.

COUNSELLOR REFRAME: You've described the way you see your husband pushing you away and not being prepared to talk to you, and that hurts you terribly. I am wondering if it is possible that maybe your husband can't cope with the emotional pressure of talking to you. I'm just wondering whether maybe what he is doing is really because of his own inadequacy, in not being able to face you. Maybe he feels guilty when he sees you, and it's easier for him to avoid seeing you altogether, rather than to tolerate his own pain. Do you think that's possible?

By tentatively putting up this alternative the client may see that there could be other reasons for her husband refusing to have anything to do with her, and that it may be that her husband is hurting and can't face the experience of seeing her. The counsellor's goal is to try to make it easier for the client to accept her husband's rejection.

Example 4

A senior executive has just described to the counsellor how terrified he is of having to stand up and address a large meeting of professionals the following week. The counsellor has reflected his feelings and allowed him, to some extent, to work through them. The counsellor then offers the following reframe:

COUNSELLOR REFRAME: It seems to me that you have mixed feelings about giving the talk. At times I almost get the impression that you are looking forward to it, and yet you say that you are very anxious about it. I am wondering if it would be possible for you to think of your anxiety as blocked excitement. Sometimes anxiety is due to us stopping ourselves from being excited, and if we let go and allow ourselves to be enthusiastic and excited, then the excitement can overshadow the anxiety.

The counsellor here is using a useful reframe from Gestalt Therapy by reframing "anxiety" as "blocked excitement". Very often, holding our emotional selves in and putting restraints on ourselves prevents us from enjoying the exciting parts of our lives as we negatively reframe exciting events as anxious moments. A good example of this is the way a bride may prepare for her wedding. One way of thinking about going through the wedding ceremony and the reception is to say "Wow, that's a really anxiety-producing situation". Another way of looking at it, a reframe, is to say "Wow, this is going to be a really exciting day and it's going to be fun". I noticed my own daughter on her wedding day as she replaced anxiety by excitement.

Example 5

The client explains how he is frequently being hurt by the boss who ignores him. The boss doesn't even look at him and she doesn't say "Hello" when she meets him in the morning. She walks straight past him.

COUNSELLOR REFRAME: You've explained to me how your boss walks straight past you without noticing you, and I'm wondering if there is an alternative explanation for what's happening. Sure, it may be that she really does intend to snub you. On the other hand, is it possible that she gets terribly preoccupied and really isn't on this planet half the time.

In this reframe, the counsellor is presenting an alternative which may be partly true. It's quite likely that the boss is sometimes preoccupied, and that may be a partial explanation. By putting this possible explanation up as an alternative, some of the sting is taken out of the boss ignoring the client, and the client may then feel less uptight in his relationship with her.

Example 6

The client explained to the counsellor his feelings of inadequacy and failure. He knew that he was intellectually bright and that made him feel worse because he never completed any project which he started. He would start enthusiastically and soon lose interest. He was deeply depressed by a long string of past "failures", things that he had started and then left half finished. COUNSELLOR REFRAME: You seem to be a very intelligent person who is quite capable of completing any of the projects which you have started. My guess is that you are excited by new projects because they present a challenge, and that you lose interest only when you believe that the challenge is easy for you to meet. Because you are highly intelligent you very quickly get bored and look for new stimulation.

This reframe enables the client to feel good about himself instead of perceiving himself as a failure. He is then left with the possibility that he can decide to do the boring thing and complete a project if he wishes, or can choose to continue looking for excitement and stimulation without feeling so guilty.

As you can see, reframing needs to be done carefully, sensitively and tentatively. If it is done in this way, it is likely to be accepted by the client. Sometimes though, the client may not think that your reframe fits his picture. However, by being offered an alternative way of viewing things he may be able to broaden his perspective with a resulting reduction in his hurt and pain.

Before reading the next chapter, practise reframing by using the following examples of client statements. If you are in a training group discuss and compare your reframes with those of other group members. Some suggested reframes for these examples are provided at the end of this chapter.

Practice examples for reframing

Example 1

CLIENT STATEMENT: I can't believe something so terrible should happen. My husband has been granted custody of my children and I'm only allowed to see them on alternate weekends. He claims that I can't cope with them, and I feel like a total failure because in some ways he's right. They used to drive me crazy. But I love them and want to have a good relationship with them. Now I'll have so little contact with them, they'll hardly know me.

Example 2

CLIENT STATEMENT: I crave for a long-term relationship with someone, and all I get is short relationship after short relationship. I just don't seem to be able to hold on to my lady-friends. They always criticize me for being so restless and for never relaxing, and none of them want to stay with me.

Example 3

CLIENT STATEMENT: My father hates me, I'm sure. He picks on me for everything I do. All the time he follows me around and complains about my behaviour. He wants me to behave like a toffy-nosed snob instead of a normal human being. Not only that but he's always nagging me to study more!

Example 4

CLIENT STATEMENT: I've got so much that I have to do in a day and I get so angry with myself because I keep making mistakes. Sure, I get lots done, but I keep forgetting things and mixing arrangements up. I'm hopeless. When will I learn?

Example 5

CLIENT STATEMENT: I'm furious with my mother. She lets my sister, Annette, manipulate her with suicide threats and her refusal to eat properly. Mum rushes around attending to her every need. It's just not fair on Mum and I wish she'd stop doing it.

Example 6

CLIENT STATEMENT: My son's unemployed again, and I resent having to support him financially. Why should I spend my money on a person who's mean and nasty to me? It would serve him right if I let him starve. What annoys me is that he knows that he can treat me badly and then twist me around his little finger and I will support him. I'm angry at myself for being so stupid as to be manipulated so easily.

Suggested reframes for practice examples

Example 1 reframe

(This reframe would be used only after fully reflecting and working through the client's distress in the usual way.) Maybe when you do see your children now you'll be able to have some quality time with them, and will be able to recharge yourself and do something for yourself in the time when they are not with you.

Example 2 reframe

You must be very attractive to the opposite sex to be able to build so many new relationships. By the sound of it, you have plenty of energy, and I wonder whether the woman friends you've had would have been able to satisfy you for very long?

Example 3 reframe

I get the impression that your father wants you to be socially and educationally successful. Maybe he actually cares about you so much that he worries in case you fail in life.

Example 4 reframe

People who do nothing never make mistakes. Making mistakes could be a sign that you are, to use your words, "getting lots done". You could feel good about that.

Example 5 reframe

Your mother must care a great deal about Annette to choose to do what she does.

Example 6 reframe

You must be a very caring person to choose to support your son, especially as you don't like his behaviour much.

Further reading on reframing

Bandler, R. and Grinder, J. *Reframing—Neuro-Linguistic Programming and the Transformation of Meaning.* Moab: Real People Press, 1982.

12 Confrontation

What do you feel emotionally when you decide to confront someone? Probably apprehension and concern about the outcome of your confrontation. What is it like for you when someone confronts you? Is it sometimes threatening? It probably is.

Generally when we use the word "confrontation" we think in terms of opposing parties and of people disagreeing as they confront each other. In such a situation the person being confronted is likely to feel threatened and may become defensive, while the person doing the confronting is likely to feel anxiety.

Confrontation as a counselling skill is somewhat different from the generally perceived view of confrontation although it is in some ways similar. The micro-skill of confrontation involves raising the awareness of the client by presenting to him information which in some way he is overlooking or failing to identify for himself. Correct use of this skill involves bringing into the client's awareness, in an acceptable way, information which may be unpalatable to him and which is either being avoided or is just not being noticed.

How do you help a child to swallow foul-tasting medicine? You can either force it down his throat, or use a more gentle persuasive approach. The problem with trying to force the medicine down is that the child may well vomit it up and your relationship with him will not be improved. Respecting the child's feelings is likely to have a more positive outcome than ignoring them. Similarly clients deserve a high degree of respect, and they usually don't like being told painful truths. Metaphorically speaking, the art of good confrontation is to help the client to swallow "bad medicine" voluntarily, so that he can incorporate it into his bodily system and digest it.

Confrontation is clearly a difficult skill to master and should not be attempted until the skills which have previously been described in this book have become a natural part of your counselling style. The skills which you have learnt already are often sufficient in themselves, making confrontation unnecessary.

Before using confrontation look within yourself to examine your feelings, motives and goals. Ask yourself "Do I want to confront because I am impatient and not prepared to allow the client to move at his own pace; do I want to confront because I just enjoy confrontation; am I wanting to use confrontation to put my own values onto the client; or am I feeling angry

with the client and wanting to express my anger through confrontation?". If the answer to any of these questions is "Yes", then confrontation is inappropriate. Satisfying the counsellor's own needs is no justification for confrontation. Confrontation should only be used after the use of other micro-skills has failed to sufficiently increase the client's awareness.

There are a number of situations in which confrontation is appropriate. For example confrontation is appropriate where:

1. the client is avoiding a basic issue which appears to be troubling him;
2. the client is failing to recognize his own self-destructive or self-defeating behaviour;
3. the client is failing to recognize possible serious consequences of his behaviour;
4. the client is out of touch with reality;
5. the client is making self-contradictory statements;
6. the client is excessively and inappropriately locked into talking about the past or the future and is unable to focus on the present;
7. the client is going around in circles by repeating the same story over and over like a cracked record;
8. the client's non-verbal behaviour does not match his verbal behaviour;
9. attention needs to be given to what is going on in the relationship between the client and counsellor, for example where dependency is occurring, or where a client withdraws or shows anger or some other emotion towards the counsellor.

In situations such as these, the counsellor may confront the client by sharing with the client what he feels, notices or observes. Good confrontation usually includes elements of some or all of the following:

1. A reflection or brief summary of what the client has said, so that the client feels heard and understood.
2. A statement of the counsellor's present feelings.
3. A concrete statement of what the counsellor has noticed or observed given without interpretation.

In addition to the above, good confrontation is presented in such a way that the client can feel OK about himself rather than attacked or put down. These points are best explained by means of examples.

Examples to illustrate the use of confrontation

Example 1

The client had been referring obliquely to his concerns about his sexuality. He mentioned the sexual problem briefly several times and then immediately deflected away from it by talking about seemingly irrelevant trivia.

COUNSELLOR CONFRONTATION: I'm puzzled because I've noticed that several times you've briefly mentioned your sexual problem, and then have started talking about something quite different.

COMMENT: Notice how the counsellor first expressed his feelings by saying "I'm puzzled", and then gave a concrete statement of what he had noticed occurring. This response is minimally threatening as it merely feeds back to the client what the counsellor has observed, without judgment.

Example 2

An angry separated husband who had been denied custody of his children was threatening to burn down the matrimonial home when his wife and children were out. Even though he had been asked about possible consequences he failed to recognize the serious consequences of his threat. The counsellor had reflected back the client's anger and attitude towards his wife. This had reduced the client's anger level but he still felt excessively vindictive and admitted to this.

COUNSELLOR CONFRONTATION: You are so furious with your wife that you want to hurt her by destroying the family home. I'm very concerned when I hear you threatening to do this because you would hurt your wife, your children, and yourself. Clearly, if you were to burn down the house your children would lose their home and possessions, and you might end up in jail.

COMMENT: Notice how the counsellor first reflected back the feelings and content of the client's message, followed this by a statement of his own feelings, and completed the confrontation by giving a factual statement of likely consequences. This latter statement was not a statement of the counsellor's opinion, but was an accurate statement of the likely consequences.

There is also an ethical issue here. Where people or property could be injured or damaged the counsellor has a responsibility to prevent this from occurring. After reading Chapter 25, I suggest that you discuss the issue of confidentiality in a situation such as this with your training group or supervisor.

Example 3

The client had come to the counsellor as a result of a crisis in her current personal relationship with a longstanding close friend. The counsellor helped her to explore past events at length, as she chose to do that. It seemed to the counsellor that nothing further would be achieved by continuing to focus on the past. However, although the client said that she wanted to talk about her present crisis, she continually recounted past events.

COUNSELLOR CONFRONTATION: I am puzzled. My impression is that you want to resolve your present crisis and yet you continually talk about past events. Unfortunately, the past can't be changed but what you can change is what is happening in the present.

COMMENT: The response started with a statement of the counsellor's feelings, "I'm puzzled", followed by a reflection of the client's desire to talk about her present crisis, and then a concrete statement of what the counsellor had observed: "You continually talk about past events". In this example the counsellor adds another factual statement which might be useful for the client: "Unfortunately the past can't be changed, but what you can change is what is happening in the present".

Remember that it is appropriate for clients to deal with past events in a constructive way where those events are significantly influencing present thoughts and feelings. However, the suggested confrontation would be appropriate where a client was inappropriately and excessively using past history to avoid facing present problems.

Example 4

Here is an example of a counsellor response that addresses repetitive behaviour by a client, who kept repeating himself by going over and over the same ground.

COUNSELLOR CONFRONTATION: I've noticed that we seem to be going round in circles, so I'll summarize what we've talked about . . . (the end of this statement is a summary).

COMMENT: This example demonstrates how the client was confronted with his repetitive behaviour. The counsellor first told the client what he had noticed happening, and then gave a summary. By confronting in this way, a counsellor can increase the client's awareness of what is happening and that increase in awareness may be sufficient to help him to move out of the rut in which he is stuck. However sometimes, even after confrontation, the client will persist in going around the track again and repeating the same details. It is here that heavier confrontation is needed and the counsellor might say

"I'm starting to feel frustrated, because once again we are going around the same track".

Example 5

The client said "I feel really happy in my marriage", using a very depressed tone of voice and slumping down in her chair as she spoke.

COUNSELLOR CONFRONTATION: I noticed that your voice sounded very flat and you slumped down in your chair when you said that you felt really happy in your marriage.

COMMENT: Here the counsellor confronted by reflecting back what he observed without putting an interpretation on his observation. The client was then free to make her own interpretation of the feedback given.

In summary, confrontation is the art of increasing the client's awareness by giving him information which he is unaware of himself, in an acceptable form. Confrontation is best done caringly, sparingly and skilfully!

13 Challenging self-destructive beliefs

Every person is entitled to his own belief system, and has the right to choose what he will believe and what he won't. It is not the counsellor's role or right to try to change the client's beliefs, but it is a counsellor's responsibility to raise the client's awareness of his choices.

Sometimes clients have self-destructive beliefs or S.D.B.s for short. There are two major categories of S.D.B. These are:

1. Should, must, or ought beliefs.
2. Irrational beliefs.

Consider the first category, that is, the "should", "must" or "ought" beliefs. Clients often make statements using the words "I should", "I must" or "I ought". Sometimes the words are spoken with enthusiasm, firmness and meaning, and it is clear that the client feels good about doing whatever it is that he "should do", "must do" or "ought to do", and that's OK. At other times the words are spoken in an unconvincing way, as though some other person is saying to the client "you should", or "you must", or "you ought", and the client is reluctantly, uncomfortably and maybe resentfully accepting that message. When this occurs, the client is likely to feel confused and emotionally disturbed. If he does as the "should" message tells him, he may feel like a small boy reluctantly and miserably doing as he is told by others. He will not feel in control of his life, and he will not recognize his behaviour as being of his own choosing. If, on the other hand, he disregards the "should" message, he feels guilty, with consequent negative results for himself. The goal of counselling, in such instances is to help the person to feel more in harmony with his decisions, so that when he makes a choice he does it willingly, and without feelings of either resentment or guilt. Provided that underlying issues are correctly and fully addressed this goal is usually achievable.

Let us now think about where should, must and ought messages come from. As children we grow up in a world in which we have no experience. We do not know the difference between right and wrong, and we cannot distinguish good behaviour from bad behaviour. However, we learn, initially from our parents and close family, and then from others such as teachers, religious leaders, and friends. We learn from the people who care for us, from what they tell us verbally, and by watching and copying their behaviour, and so gradually we absorb a system of values, attitudes, and beliefs. It is right and proper that we do so.

As we grow through childhood and adolescence there comes a time when we start to challenge and rebel against some of the beliefs which we have absorbed from others. Interestingly though, many people, by the time they are young adults, hold onto most of the beliefs and values of their parents whilst having rejected some. As children it is clearly appropriate that we should learn and absorb the beliefs of our parents and significant others. There is no other way for us to learn, because as children our experience is too limited for us to make mature judgments for ourselves. As adults, we do have that experience and it is appropriate for each of us to determine for ourselves which beliefs fit and make sense for us as individuals and which beliefs do not fit. We can then keep what fits and reject that which does not, replacing the unfitting by something new and fitting (see Satir, 1975).

Sometimes when a client uses the words should, must, or ought, he is stating a belief that has its origins in his childhood, and which he is holding on to, but which does not fit for him now. If he really accepted the belief as his own he would be more likely to say "I've decided that", or "I want to", or "I choose to", rather than "I should", or "I must", or "I ought". Of course I am describing the general case and this is not always true. What is important is to encourage the client to own his choices as being morally right and fitting for him, rather than for him to attribute his decisions to an external moral code which is being imposed on him by others or through childhood conditioning.

The problem with shoulds, musts and oughts is that often the words spoken are believed at a head or thinking level, but do not sit comfortably at a gut or feeling level. Where there is a mismatch between what is happening at a head level and what is being experienced at a gut level, the person will be confused and emotionally distressed. Human beings are holistic beings, so we cannot separate our emotional feelings, our bodily sensations, our thoughts and our spiritual experiences into discrete compartments. They all interrelate and must be in harmony with each other if we are to feel integrated and comfortable.

When I listen to a client who uses an "I should" statement and then expresses reluctance to do what he believes he "should" do, then I try to raise the client's awareness of what is happening within him in such a way that he becomes more fully aware of his options and can, if he chooses, challenge his own "I should" message. He may then decide that the message fits for him and accept it more willingly, or he may decide that it does not fit and so replace it with a different message. I explain to the client where many "I should" messages come from, and ask him where he thinks his particular "I should" message came from. I encourage him to check out whether the message sits comfortably with him. If it does, that is great! If it doesn't then maybe he can replace it with something more fitting. A similar approach can be used when helping clients to challenge "ought" or "must" statements.

Apart from "shoulds", "musts" and "oughts", other S.D.B.s include what Albert Ellis, the originator of Rational Emotive Therapy, refers to as irrational beliefs. Like "shoulds", "musts", and "oughts", irrational beliefs are often absorbed from others during our childhood. Irrational beliefs often include the words "should", "must", or "ought". These words may be applied by the speaker to himself but in the case of irrational beliefs are also frequently applied to others in statements such as "Other people should . . ." Table 1 gives some examples of common irrational beliefs and rational alternatives. Notice how the irrational belief is certain to make the client feel bad whereas the rational alternative helps him to feel good.

For other examples of irrational beliefs see Chapter 20.

If your client verbalizes an irrational belief, encourage him to question it by asking a question yourself. For example, you might ask "Is it realistic to expect that life will be fair and just?". By doing this the client is very likely to challenge his own S.D.B., that life should be fair and just. If he does so, you may suggest a rational alternative.

You may wish to explain the difference between rational and irrational beliefs to your client and to point out that irrational beliefs inevitably make people feel bad. You can then encourage your client to write down a list of his irrational beliefs and replace them by rational alternatives. Remember that a client has the right to retain his irrational beliefs if he wishes. It is his choice, so do not attempt to persuade him to change, just raise his awareness of the consequences of irrational beliefs.

As with confronting, skill and care are needed when challenging S.D.B.s. Ideally the challenge will come from the client rather than from you the counsellor. However, it can be helpful for a client if you explain to him the nature, origin and effects of S.D.B.s, so that he is able to recognize and challenge them.

The ideas expressed in this chapter have their origin in Rational Emotive Therapy, although, in contrast to the approach described here, Rational Emotive Therapists are direct in their efforts to challenge and persuade their clients. If such an approach appeals to you then you may wish to learn more about Rational Emotive Therapy once you have mastered basic counselling skills.

Table 1 Comparison between rational and irrational beliefs

Irrational belief	Rational alternative
I must never make mistakes.	The only way not to make mistakes is to do nothing. I'm active, and all active people make mistakes.
Other people should not make mistakes.	No-one's perfect. I can accept that other people will make mistakes.
Other people make me angry.	I make myself angry when I don't accept that other people don't live up to my expectations.
Other people should live up to my expectations.	Other people don't need to live up to my expectations.
My happiness depends on other people's behaviour and attitudes.	My happiness comes from within me and does not depend on others.
I must live up to other people's expectations.	I don't need to live up to other people's expectations to be OK.
I must win.	According to the law of averages most people only win 50 per cent of the time. I don't need to win to feel OK.
Life should be fair and just.	Life is not fair and just.
I must get my own way.	I do not need to get my own way to feel OK, and I can sometimes get satisfaction out of letting other people have their own way.
I need other people's approval to feel OK.	It's nice to get other people's approval, but I do not need their approval to feel OK.
I must always please other people.	It's unrealistic to expect that I can always please other people.
I must never get angry.	It's OK to be angry sometimes.
I should always be happy.	There is a time to be happy and a time to be sad.
I must not cry.	It's OK to cry.
I can't be happy if people misjudge me.	People sometimes will misjudge me. That's inevitable. But I know that I'm OK and that's what matters.

Further reading on challenging self-destructive beliefs

Bernard, M. E. *Staying Rational in an Irrational World.* Melbourne: Macmillan, 1986.

Dyer, W. W. *Your Erroneous Zones.* London: Sphere, 1976.

Ellis, A. and Bernard, M. E. (eds). *Clinical Applications of Rational-Emotive Therapy.* New York: Plenum, 1975.

Ellis, A. and Harper, R. A. *A New Guide to Rational Living.* Hollywood: Wilshire Book Company, 1975.

14   Exploring options

When a client comes to see a counsellor it is often because the client feels hopelessly stuck in an intolerable situation, in which she does not know what to do to ease her pain, and believes that there is no apparent solution to her problems. This hopeless feeling may lock the client into depression, anxiety, and tension. Use of the reflective and other skills which have been described previously enables the client to explore her issues and to clarify them. This process alone may be helpful in reducing her distress, and she may spontaneously move towards exploring options for herself and finding solutions for her problems. Sometimes however, the client does not move forwards in this way and appears to reach an impasse, without properly exploring her options. An appropriate way for the counsellor to deal with this situation is to reflect the feeling of being "stuck" and then to ask the client what her options are. This can be done by asking an open question such as "You are obviously in a very uncomfortable situation. What do you see as your options?". By asking this question, rather than suggesting options, the counsellor encourages the client to take responsibility for solving her own problems. The client is then able to think about and suggest options for consideration. Some of these options she will, almost certainly, immediately discard as impossible. However, be careful to remember all the options that the client suggests because an option which the client has ruled out initially may turn out to be the one which she will eventually choose.

New counsellors often feel pressured into trying to find options for their clients. My experience is that generally, it is not necessary to do this, and that it is far better if clients are able to come up with their own options. Of course there are times, when for some reason, a client fails to see an option which is obvious to the counsellor, and in such a case the counsellor may choose to tell the client about that option. However, when a counsellor does put forward an idea of her own, it's preferable that it should be put forward in a tentative way, so that the client sees it as nothing more than a possible suggestion and does not take it as advice.

When exploring options, let the client talk in a general way about the various alternatives and then summarize them clearly. Encourage the client to explore each idea individually and to talk about the positive and negative aspects of each option. There are some advantages in dealing with the most unlikely or least preferred options first. Thus, the client gets these out of the way, and this leaves her with a smaller range of options, which makes it easier for her to move towards a final decision.

Encourage the client not only to look carefully at the consequences, both negative and positive, of each option, but also to take into account her own gut feelings about the various alternatives that are available. Quite often a person's logical thinking will be pulling her in one direction whereas her gut feelings will be pulling her in a different direction. It is, for example, quite common to hear a client say "That is what I really ought to do, that is what I should do, but I don't want to do that, it doesn't feel right for me". Obviously the client needs to feel very comfortable with the decision that she makes, or she is unlikely to stay with it. Logical thinking alone does not provide sufficient grounds on which to choose an option. In fact, I believe that it's more important for the client to feel comfortable at a gut level with an option, than for her to think that the option is the most sensible one. However, any option chosen obviously has to be the client's choice and may not be the choice which the counsellor believes to be the most desirable, sensible or appropriate.

Imagine that your client is in a dilemma and is unable to make a choice between two options, option A and option B. In order for the client to resolve her dilemma, help her to fully explore what it would feel like to have chosen option A, and to explore what the consequences of this choice would be. After this is completed encourage her to do a similar exploration for option B. This enables a clear comparison between the two options to be established.

One of the problems in making a choice between two alternatives is that whenever we make a choice, almost invariably there is a loss or cost involved. Let me give you an example. I'm actually writing this on a Saturday, a nice sunny Saturday in Queensland, Australia. I have two options. One option is to continue writing and the other option is to stop work and to go down to the beach for a swim, and so I have a dilemma. Which should I do? I enjoy writing and quite enjoy what I am doing now, but it would also be fun to go down to the beach and swim. Now that's not a heavy choice, but whichever choice I make will involve a loss. If I decide to keep on writing then I lose out on the exercise, the fresh air and the fun of being down at the beach, but if I go down to the beach I'll have a different loss. I'll lose the satisfaction of continuing to do something creative, that is, my writing, and I'll feel frustrated by not having made more progress with my writing when tomorrow comes. So, whether I continue to write or whether I go to the beach, I have to accept that there is a loss either way. If I choose one alternative I lose the other. One of the main blocks in decision-making occurs when people don't properly look at the loss or cost component in their decision-making. Frequently I discover that accepting the loss or cost

associated with a decision is more difficult than choosing between the positive aspects of the two choices. It can be very helpful to tell a client about the loss or cost component in decision-making, and to explain it as it applies to her particular dilemma. Ask the client, "If you choose option A, what are your losses going to be?" and "If you choose option B, what are your losses going to be?". Ask her whether she would be able to accept those losses. The choice is not just a choice between two positives, but also a choice which involves choosing between two losses and deciding which loss is acceptable, if either. By focusing on the loss or cost component as well as the positive component of options, clients are more readily able to make decisions and resolve their dilemmas.

Resolution of dilemmas is difficult for most people. Part of that difficulty is due to the polarities that exist within us. Let me go back to my previous example where I looked at the dilemma of continuing to write or going to the beach. Right now it is as though there are two parts of me. One part of me wants to go to the coast and have a swim, and the other part of me wants to stay here and continue writing this book. I have found that it is very helpful for clients if I describe their dilemmas in terms of parts of themselves. Sometimes I say to a client, "Part of you wants to make choice A and another part of you wants to make choice B. These are both valid parts of you. They both exist in you at the same time". I ask the client to tell me about the part of her that wants option "A" and to explore that part fully, and then to tell me about the part of her that wants option "B" and to explore that fully. By doing this, I allow the client to integrate and own two opposite parts of herself and not to feel confused, but rather to accept that both are valid parts of herself (see Chapter 19 which deals with parts of self). The client is then empowered to accept that choosing one of the options means letting go of the other option, and that involves a cost or the acceptance of a loss, the loss of the option which is not chosen. Most people have been taught as children that there is always a correct choice, and that in dilemmas the choice of one option is correct and the choice of the other is wrong. Confusion often arises from the unrealistic expectation that choice involves a decision between black and white, or between right and wrong. In reality, most human decisions involve deciding between shades of grey where both options have advantages or positive qualities and both have costs or disadvantages.

Remember, if I choose option A, I lose option B, and that loss is part of the cost of choosing option A. To resolve a dilemma, and choose one option, I have to let go of the other. The letting go is the hard part. Let your client know that and she will be more easily able to reach a decision.

Sometimes a client will stay stuck and will be unable to resolve a dilemma even though the issues are clearly understood. As a new counsellor, I often felt panicky when a client was stuck and would sometimes prolong a counselling session unnecessarily in an effort to try to unstick the client and lead the client to a satisfying solution. I now realize that such counsellor behaviour is very inadvisable. It is much more helpful to reflect back to the client her stuckness, to say "Look, it seems as though we've come to an impasse. There doesn't seem to be an easy solution, and today you seem to be stuck and just don't know which way to go. Let's leave it there. Come back another time and we will talk together again". By saying this, the counsellor gives the client permission to remain stuck, takes the panic out of the situation, and lets the client know that she, the counsellor, still cares and is prepared to work with the client again. Sometimes the client will come back the next time saying "I've made a decision", because she was given permission to stay stuck and effectively given time to think through what was discussed in the previous session without pressure. At other times a client will remain stuck. Then the counsellor's goal is to assist her to come to terms with the consequences of being stuck in a painful or uncomfortable situation. The counsellor does this by assisting the client to verbalize her feelings about being stuck, and then encouraging her to talk about how she will cope with her stuckness.

In the next chapter we will try to develop a deeper understanding of the process required to help clients deal with blocks to decision-making. However, before proceeding to the next chapter please make sure that you have fully grasped the idea that it is OK to allow a client to remain "stuck". Often experiencing being stuck for a while is necessary before progress can be made.

15 Facilitating action

By using the micro-skills described in the previous chapters an effective counsellor will enable the client to move out of confusion and anxiety, and into a more comfortable emotional space. If that is achieved, then the client has clearly been helped by the counselling process in the short term, and for some clients that is sufficient. However, for many clients, their emotional distress is a consequence of entrenched life situations, and unless action is taken to change those life situations then emotional distress will inevitably return.

Some clients exhibit the "cracked record" syndrome. They go to see a counsellor again and again, with the same unresolved problem. The experienced counsellor needs to have the necessary skills to assist such clients to move forward by making specific and observable changes to their life situations.

Have you ever experienced resistance from a person when you have tried to persuade her to make useful life changes for herself? We human beings are rather like the proverbial donkey. The more someone pushes or pulls us the more we tend to resist! If I am to enable a person to take action to change then I must resist the temptation to push for change and must use a different strategy. The strategy which I need to use is admirably described in Gestalt Therapy theory (see Zinker, 1977).

A modified version of the *Gestalt awareness circle* is shown in Figure 3.

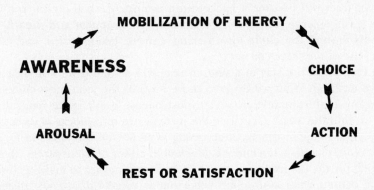

Figure 3. Awareness Circle.

An understanding of this circle will enable you, the counsellor, to help your clients to move into action spontaneously when they have progressed through the necessary preliminary steps. We will now look at the awareness circle in some detail starting at the point of *arousal*.

Clients generally come for counselling when they are emotionally distressed. That is, when they are at the *arousal* point on the *awareness circle*, with their emotions unpleasantly aroused. The counsellor's task is to enable the client to move around the circle towards *satisfaction* or *rest*. This is achieved by raising the client's AWARENESS.

In the *arousal* phase, the emotionally disturbed client is unable to focus clearly, and sees a confused picture of her world. It is as though she were looking at an overgrown forest, choked by too many trees and much undergrowth. She is unable to clearly see any one tree, but instead is overwhelmed by a blurred and confusing picture. In this state, the client's energy is depleted. She will be unable to see her options, and will therefore have little hope of taking any action to change her situation.

If the client is to feel better, she needs to *mobilize her energy* so that she can work constructively to resolve her issues. The counsellor can facilitate this mobilization of energy by raising the client's awareness of her inner experiences. As a trainee counsellor, if you have mastered the skills described in the previous chapters, then you have the tools required to do this. By using these micro-skills you will inevitably raise the client's awareness, and consequently will *mobilize her energy*.

As you progress in your training you will learn more advanced skills which will enhance your capabilities as a counsellor by speeding up the awareness process. However the skills you have already, are sufficient if you use them effectively.

Sometimes, once awareness is raised, the client will move with ease around the awareness circle. To use the previous analogy, the overgrown forest of trees will become a background against which the clear outline of one tree will emerge. The client's confusion will disappear and she will move naturally around the circle into making a *choice*, taking *action*, and coming into a state of *satisfaction* or *rest*.

In life, we do not stay in a state of rest, and if we did we would probably achieve nothing. What we do is to move around the awareness circle again and again. Unfortunately, however, most people don't move naturally and easily around the awareness circle but instead run into blocks as discussed in the previous chapter. Blocks often occur, as shown on the circle in Figure 4, before *choice* or *action*. If a client is blocked in either of these places, then it is tempting for the counsellor to focus on encouraging her to make a choice or to take action. Such counsellor behaviour is usually disastrous. Instead of achieving the counsellor's goal of helping the client to make a choice or to

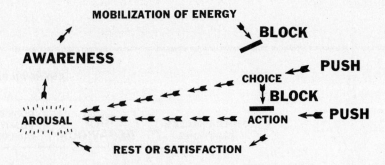

Figure 4. The effect of pushing for choice or action.

take action, pushing for choice or action returns the client to an even higher state of arousal (see the arrows in Figure 4).

If you want to help your client to make a choice or to take action, then a prerequisite is to enable the client to work through any block which might be impeding progress around the circle. Whenever a client is blocked and unable to make a choice or take action, resist the temptation to push the client into doing so, and instead return to the awareness point on the circle. Raise the client's awareness of her block and encourage her to explore how it feels to be blocked and unable to move forwards. Encourage her to become aware of what she is experiencing internally. Ask her what messages she is getting from her body, from her emotional feelings, and from her thoughts, when she experiences her inability to decide or act. This enables her to explore and to deal with the block, which may free her to move around the circle to a more comfortable position. It is also possible that, by dealing with her block, she may discover that she has another more important issue which needs confronting.

Remember, the more you push a client to make a choice or to take action, the more blocked she is likely to become. If you want to help her to move on then you need to raise her awareness of the block.

Suitable questions to help clients explore blocks are as follows:

1. Tell me what you are experiencing emotionally as you think about making this decision (or taking this action)?
2. What are you aware of happening inside you when you think about making a choice (or taking action)?

Taking action involves change, and change can be scary. The most common blocks which inhibit action are identified in the simple dilemma model in Figure 5.

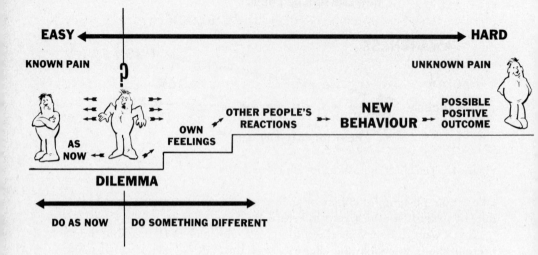

Figure 5.   Dilemma model.

A client who makes decisions and takes action to change her life has to cope firstly with her own feelings, and then with other people's reactions. This is often difficult, particularly if the decisions or actions displease others. Also, if a client does something new, then she takes a risk; there may be unknown consequences, and these could be painful. It may be easier to go on living as now, with no changes and with known pain, rather than to take a risk and do something new and different with its unknown pain. Thus it is easy to understand how client choices and actions are often blocked by internal fears and anxieties.

Blocks to choice and action include the following:

- inability to deal with own feelings.
- inability to cope with the reactions of others.
- fear of consequences.
- fear of a repetition of past bad experiences.
- the intrusion of inappropriate shoulds, musts, and oughts.
- fear that something comfortable or rewarding will be lost.
- lack of skills to carry out the desired action.

In summary, for most clients, if you the counsellor use the micro-skills which you have learnt to raise AWARENESS and to work through blocks, then the client is likely to move spontaneously around the awareness circle, to make *choices* and to take the necessary *action* to achieve goals. However, for some clients this approach alone is not sufficient.

Clients with the "cracked record" syndrome may, if they are permitted, repeatedly use the counselling process to enable them to continue to exist in unsatisfactory life situations without change. If this happens, then they are likely to sink further into despair and hopelessness. Such clients need specific help in facilitating action, if they are to bring about meaningful changes to their lives. Also, there are some clients who, after deciding what they want to do, find themselves unable to move forwards into action, not because of psychological blocks, but rather because they do not have the necessary skills or confidence to carry out the action which they wish to take. These clients need additional help. The rest of this chapter deals with ways of helping clients who do not have the necessary confidence or personal resources to make and implement action plans on their own.

Clearly, it is not helpful for a counsellor to do the client's work. By doing that, the counsellor would reinforce the client's sense of helplessness, and lead the client to believe that she needed to have assistance each time new goals were to be targeted. What is helpful is for the client to learn how to organize, to plan, and to execute decisions so that in the future she is able to do these things for herself. A good way of helping her to learn is to walk alongside her, and to work with her as she struggles with the issues involved in achieving one important goal. You can then if you wish explore with her the processes used in achieving her goal. Thus she may identify those processes which were most useful to her so that she can use them in achieving future goals.

Although every situation is different, there are some basic steps which are useful in enabling clients to take action to achieve goals. These steps are listed in the action plan below.

Action plan

1. Make psychological preparation;
2. Identify the goal;
3. Identify the first step towards goal achievement;
4. Concretize the first step towards goal achievement;
5. Decide how to carry out the first step;
6. Acquire the skills to carry out the first step;
7. Decide when to carry out the first step;
8. Carry out the first step;
9. Reward self for achieving the first step;
10. Reassess overall goal.

We will now look in detail at these steps in the order presented above. In order to make the exercise more meaningful consider the specific example of a father who has a dysfunctional relationship with his teenage son.

1. Psychological preparation

This has been dealt with earlier in this chapter. The counsellor raises client awareness, to enable the client to work through blocks and to come to a decision.

2. Identifying the goal

Imagine that the father in our example had come to the decision that he wanted to work on improving his relationship with his son. For many clients, identifying such a goal would be sufficient to facilitate action, and the counsellor's work would be over. For other clients, further help would be needed.

3. Identifying the first step towards goal achievement

For some clients, the goal of trying to improve a relationship with a son would be too broad and non-specific. It might not be clear how the goal could be achieved and consequently positive action would be unlikely to occur. Such a client needs to identify the first step towards achieving his goal. This first step needs to be realistically achievable, so that the client is likely to be rewarded by success rather than discouraged by failure.

The counsellor might ask, "How are you going to set about improving your relationship with your son ?". Maybe the father would respond, "Well, I'd like to start by having a talk with him, but that's scary, because we haven't said anything pleasant to each other for some months".

Clearly at this point the counsellor would move the focus away from the contemplated action and return to raising awareness of the client's fear of talking with his son. If this were not done then the client would be likely to be blocked from action.

4. Concretizing the first step in goal achievement

Once the first step in goal achievement has been identified, it needs to be concretized, so that it is clear and specific rather than vague. For example the statement, "I'd like to have a talk with my son" is very general. The value of such a talk is likely to depend on what the purpose of the talk is, and on what the content of the conversation is likely to be. Questions by the counsellor such as, "What do you want to say to your son?" and "What do you hope to achieve as a result of this talk?" might yield more specific information such as, "I want to tell him why I am so angry with him, so that I can get that garbage out of the way and can start relating to him in a positive way".

5. Deciding how to carry out the first step

This decision needs to take into account the likely consequences of the proposed action. For example, the statement in the paragraph above, "I want to tell him why I am so angry with him . . ." suggests that the client intends to confront his son in a way which is likely to lead to further alienation rather than reconciliation. At this point the counsellor could usefully carry out some role plays to allow the client to experience what it would be like to be the recipient of the intended message.

6. Acquiring the skills to carry out the first step

The client may need to acquire new skills in order to be able to competently carry out the first step. In our current example the counsellor might coach the client in the use of "I" statements, and carry out further role plays to determine the likely impact of client statements.

7. Deciding when to carry out step 1

Sometimes when I have to carry out an unpleasant task I will delay doing what I have decided to do by using the excuse that the time is not right. Do you do that? I think that most people do, and as a result delayed action often results in no action. I find that for me it is usually easier to carry out what I plan if I have made a clear decision about the proposed timing. I think that it's the same for many clients, and it's therefore useful to explore the issue of timing with them. This may result in more awareness raising—back to the awareness circle again!

8. Carrying out step 1

Whether or not the client carries out step 1 is unimportant. If he does, then he can feel good about that, and if he doesn't then there is a learning for him. He can once again get in touch with his inner experiences to discover what stopped him from carrying out step 1, and from that awareness a new decision can be made.

9. Rewarding self for carrying out step 1

Do you ever minimize your achievements? I sometimes do, but I am getting better at taking pride in what I am good at. Many clients fail to give themselves positive messages when they succeed in performing difficult tasks. As a counsellor help your clients to feel good about themselves by maximizing their achievements. A client who is properly rewarded for carrying out step 1 is more likely to continue making positive decisions and carrying them out.

10. Reassessing the overall goal

Often when the client has gone some way in one direction, he will realise that the goal he originally targeted is one that he no longer wants. That is clearly OK, but he will consequently need to reassess his overall goal.

In this chapter we have looked at the skills involved in facilitating action. Generally, if you use the previously learnt micro-skills and remember what you have discovered here about the *awareness circle*, you will be successful in helping clients to take appropriate action to bring about meaningful changes in their lives. Additionally, the action plan described above can be used when it is clear that the client is unable to move forward without more specific help.

16 Termination

It is often very hard for new counsellors to know when to terminate a counselling session or when to terminate a series of counselling sessions. In this chapter we will discuss the following aspects of termination:

1. The termination of an individual counselling session;
2. The need for ongoing appointments;
3. Client and counsellor dependency;
4. The termination of a series of counselling sessions.

The termination of an individual counselling session

Most counselling agencies and private practitioners schedule a particular length of time for each counselling session. It is quite common for agencies to allow one hour between each counselling appointment. Consequently the counsellor has less than an hour in which to work with each client. Between counselling sessions, the counsellor may need to make another appointment for the client who is leaving, to show the client out, to write up notes on the interview, and to read up information regarding the incoming client if such information is available. In practice, therefore, a counsellor working under such conditions has about 50 minutes to spend in the actual counselling process with each client. In my experience, this is a suitable time for most counselling sessions. Of course, there are exceptions to this rule. Sometimes it will be clear after a very short time that the interview may be terminated because the client has resolved her issues and there is little point in sitting around chatting unnecessarily. At other times it may be apparent that a client is in a highly distressed emotional state after the 50-minute session and it may be necessary to continue the interview for much longer.

Generally, it is my belief that clients tend to deal with important issues in the first three quarters of an hour of a counselling session, and that at the end of that length of time the client and counsellor begin to lose energy. It is important that each counselling session is dynamic and that the client is working actively throughout the session. Once a client becomes used to sessions being of fixed length, she will tend to work comfortably within that time frame. During a 50-minute interview a client will be likely to have raised important issues and to have explored them. The client then needs time in which to process the work which has been done. It may therefore be appropriate to terminate the session at that point and to leave a few days, or maybe a week or two, before making another appointment, if that is needed.

If the matter is raised, let the client know that you, the counsellor, are in control of the length of the counselling session. Frequently clients show anxiety by looking at a clock in the room, because they are worried about taking up too much of a counsellor's time. In such cases it is important for the counsellor to say that she will control the length of the session, and that the session will probably last about 50 minutes, or whatever is appropriate. If a client is told this, her anxiety regarding time keeping will be reduced.

Where a counsellor is working within a set time frame, and knows that there is a time limit to the counselling session, the counsellor needs to prepare for terminating the session. This preparation should be commenced about 10 minutes before the end of the session. If the counselling session is to last 50 minutes, then after about 40 minutes the counsellor needs to assess the progress of the session. The counsellor can then decide how to use the remaining time in order to terminate in a satisfactory way for the client. It may be advisable for the counsellor to say to the client, "I am conscious of the need for us to finish the session in about 10 minutes time and it seems to me that you may wish to explore . . . (a particular area) . . . that we have been talking about". By giving the client some warning that the counselling session must end within a few minutes, the client is given an opportunity to deal with any unfinished business that needs to be completed before the end of the session. Near the finishing time, it is sometimes appropriate for the counsellor to provide a summary of the material which was discussed by the client during the session. The counsellor might also add a statement regarding goals for the future and regarding the possibility or probability of future counselling sessions being required.

The counsellor should take control of the termination of the session. She may need to be assertive, particularly with clients who want to linger on and chat rather than do useful work. In such a case, be direct and if necessary, interrupt and say something like "I realize that you would like to continue talking to me, but unfortunately that is not possible, we need to finish the session right now". Then stand up and lead the way firmly out of the room without stopping to linger, even if the client wishes to do so.

The need for ongoing appointments

Inexperienced counsellors are often apprehensive about asking clients to come back for another appointment. If you feel apprehensive about doing this, explore your feelings. You may be afraid that the client will not want to come back and will reject your offer of another appointment. If the client does do that, would it be a disaster? If you think that it would, then you need

to discuss the issue with your supervisor. Remember that it is hard for clients to make appointments. It is much easier for them to cancel out. If you don't make another appointment for the client, then she is likely to assume that you don't think it is necessary for her to come back and that you would consider it to be a nuisance if she were to do so. It is therefore important, if you do not make another appointment, that you say to your client, "I won't make another appointment for you now, because it seems to me that it's unnecessary for you to come back to see me, as your issues seem to be reasonably well resolved. However, I would like you to know that if you decide later that it would be useful for you to come back, then you are welcome to ring up and make an appointment to do that".

For clients who need ongoing appointments, it may be desirable for the counsellor to spell out an ongoing contract. It may be sufficient to say for example, "I think it would be useful for you to come back to see me again next week". Alternatively, it may be appropriate to say, "It seems to me that you have a number of issues that need to be resolved, and this is likely to take several counselling sessions. I therefore propose that you come to see me on a weekly basis for the next three or four weeks and that we then review the situation". Through this, the client is made aware of the counsellor's intention to continue seeing her.

Clients often feel insecure about the counselling relationship and are afraid that the counsellor will terminate the counselling process before important issues have been explored. It is therefore important to ensure that the client has some clear expectation regarding the possible duration of the counselling relationship.

Client and counsellor dependency

Sometimes it's desirable to terminate a series of counselling sessions sooner than the client would wish. This raises the issue of dependency. It's very easy, in fact probably inevitable, that dependency will occur in ongoing counselling relationships.

Clients are likely to become dependent on counsellors for a number of reasons. Firstly, it is inevitable that some degree of friendship will occur if the counselling relationship is genuine, warm, and accepting. Of course, that degree of friendship is controlled by the limits of the counselling relationship (see Chapter 25 on professional ethics). However, the quality of a counselling relationship is such that effective counsellors often build very meaningful relationships with their clients. It is therefore natural that clients will often want the counselling relationship to continue after its usefulness for legitimate counselling purposes has ended.

Clients tell counsellors their innermost secrets, whereas generally, from childhood, people learn to only share such private material with someone they love. There can be almost an expectation by the client, from previous life learnings, that intimate personal sharing will result in an ongoing relationship.

Some people who come to counsellors are very alone in the world, and do not have a close relative or friend with whom to share the problems and stressors which arise in their daily lives. There is good reason for such people to want to become dependent on the counselling relationship. We all have a need for some degree of closeness and affection, and the counselling relationship can provide this to the lonely, who may then become dependent on the relationship.

After the initial traumas of a crisis have passed it is often very comfortable for a client to be able to continue to discuss and work through less important life issues in the caring counselling environment. Most of us like comfort, but to continue to provide the "luxury" of counselling to clients who no longer *need* it, does them a disservice. It effectively interferes with the natural and desirable tendency of people to become self-sufficient. Effective counselling teaches clients how to work through most troubling issues on their own, and how to recognize when counselling help is really needed.

Dependency can occur in two directions. The client may become dependent on the counsellor, and equally the counsellor may become dependent on the client. Counsellors are not emotionless robots, but are human beings with emotions and needs. As described above and in Chapter 25, the counselling relationship involves an unusual degree of intimate sharing, and by its very nature involves a degree of closeness. Consequently, it is easy to understand how a counsellor can get hooked into a dependency relationship. Clearly, a counsellor needs to stay vigilant to ensure that she does not encourage her clients to continue with counselling merely to satisfy her own needs.

The termination of a series of counselling sessions

The decision about when to terminate a series of counselling sessions is often fairly clear, and will frequently be made by the client herself in discussion with the counsellor. However, there will be times when the decision is more difficult, particularly if either client or counsellor dependency is occurring. Counsellors therefore need to regularly review the progress that is being made in counselling sessions, and the goals that are being achieved, to ensure that counselling is continuing for the client's well-being, rather than for satisfying dependency needs. Where progress is not being made, and goals are not being achieved, it is unethical to encourage clients to continue.

If client dependency is identified, then the counsellor needs to bring the issue into the open, and to let the client know what she sees happening. This needs to be done with sensitivity, because it would be easy for a client to feel hurt and rejected as a consequence of inept confrontation regarding dependency. However, if the dependency is reframed positively, as a normal occurrence which involves both counsellor and client, then progress can be made towards termination.

With clients who are terminating a long counselling relationship, there will be some grief associated with the loss of that relationship. The client needs to be prepared, particularly where a long relationship has been established, for the feelings of loss that will occur when the relationship ends. In order to minimize this pain, it may be advisable for a counsellor to make one or two appointments at long intervals at the end of a series of counselling sessions. For example, when I have seen a client on a weekly basis for several weeks, I have often made the remaining appointments at fortnightly and monthly intervals.

With some clients it can be useful to have a follow-up session at the end of three months. A three-monthly follow-up session serves three purposes. Firstly, it helps the client to adjust to the idea of being independent and not dependent on the counsellor; secondly it enables the client to deal with the loss of the counselling relationship in a gentle way; and thirdly, it enables the counsellor to review the progress that the client continues to make after regular counselling has ceased. Also, it sometimes happens that after a series of counselling sessions has been completed, a three-monthly follow-up session will reveal that there is a "loose end" that needs to be tied up before final termination.

Remember, termination of both single sessions and a series of sessions is often slightly painful. It is usually difficult to say "goodbye", and accept the loss of a meaningful relationship. A counsellor needs to be aware of this, both for the client and also for herself. As discussed previously, it is important to address this issue openly and to help the client to adjust to termination. Termination needs to be done sensitively and caringly.

To terminate this chapter, here are three "don'ts". At the end of a session:

- DON'T ask the client a question;
- DON'T reflect back content;
- DON'T reflect back feelings.

If you do any of these things the session is certain to continue!

PART III
The counselling experience

17 The process of a counselling session

Each counselling session is different from every other session. No two interventions are going to be the same. However, after counselling for a long time, most counsellors find that there is a common pattern, which can often be recognized, in the processes underlying their counselling sessions. The flowchart in Figure 6 shows in diagrammatic form the processes which may evolve in a counselling session. Although this flowchart is useful in creating an understanding of the counselling process, please be aware that the various stages described by the chart will often overlap each other, repeat themselves and occur in a different order from that shown. The flowchart will be discussed in some detail in the following paragraphs under the headings shown on the right hand side of the chart.

Preparation

The counselling process starts even before the client and counsellor meet. The client, on her way to a counselling session, will usually rehearse what she intends to say. She is likely to bring with her preconceived ideas about what's going to happen in the counselling session. She will have not only expectations, but probably considerable apprehension too. Coming to a counselling session can be quite difficult for a client, because it is painful to talk about deep inner feelings, and it can be quite threatening to do this with a stranger.

The counsellor also brings her own expectations, agenda and personal feelings to the counselling session. Her expectations and agenda may be inappropriate for the client, and her personal feelings may intrude on the counselling process to the detriment of the client. The counsellor's own attitudes, beliefs and feelings are certain to influence what happens in the session. If she has personal problems of her own which are unresolved and pressing in on her, these are certain to affect her counselling. Obviously, it is very important for a counsellor to try to minimize the intrusion of her own business into the counselling process. One of the best ways for you, as a counsellor, to achieve this is to become as aware as possible of the issues that are troubling you, and as aware as possible of what you are experiencing internally during the counselling session. By being aware of what is

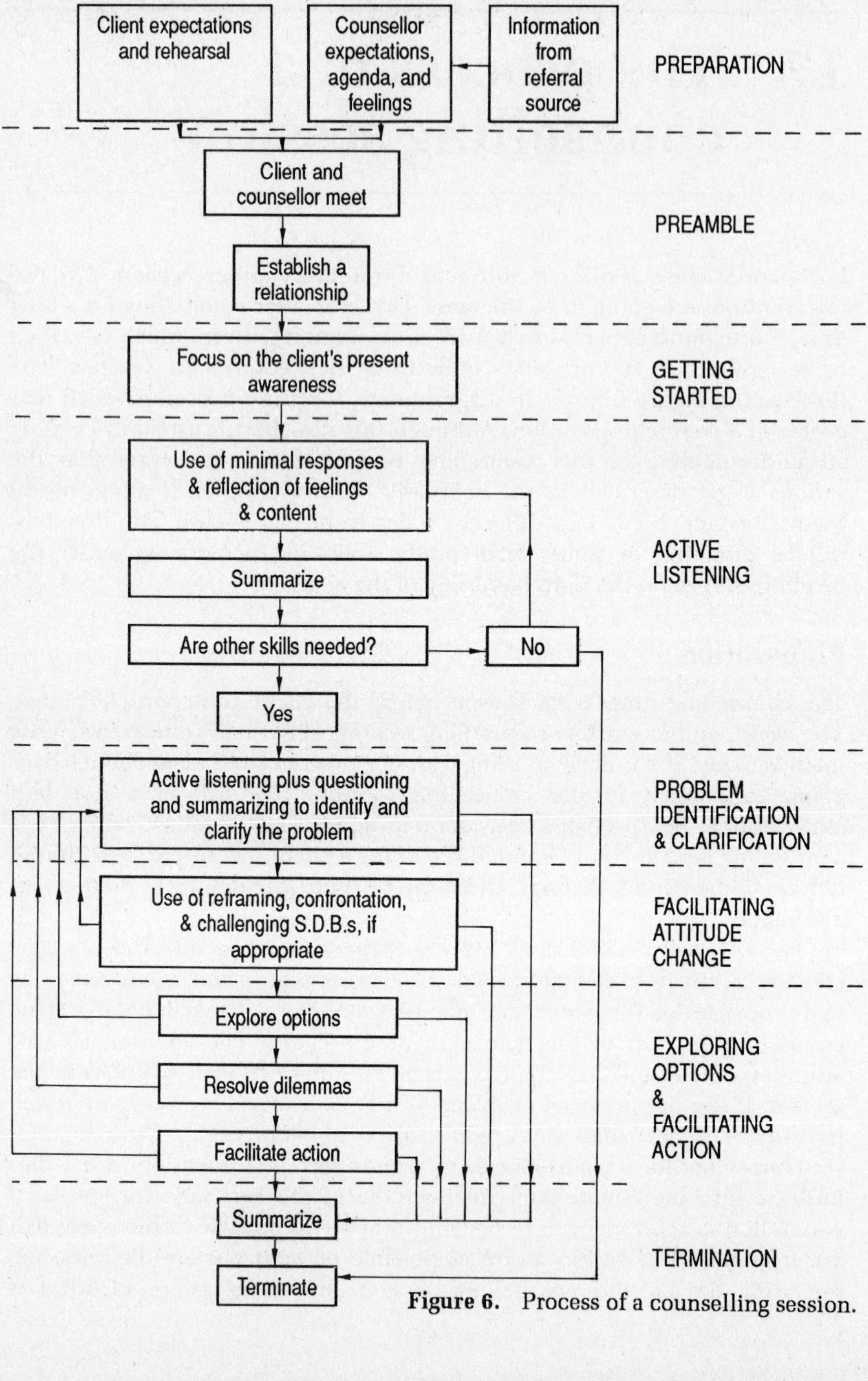

Figure 6. Process of a counselling session.

happening within yourself, you will be better able to deal appropriately with what is yours, and to separate that from what is the client's. In this way your own business will intrude less on the counselling process.

Before a counsellor has met with her client, it is possible that she may have some preconceived ideas about her. Often the counsellor will have some information before the session starts. This information may have come from the person or agency who referred the client for counselling. As a new counsellor I believed that such material often distorted my own understanding of the client. Consequently I went through a stage of trying not to listen to what referral sources told me, and of making an appointment and saying to the referral source "I'll find it all out from the client". I have changed that approach for two reasons. Firstly, I have discovered that quite often a referral source will have factual information which may take time to come out in the counselling session, and which is useful in enabling me to understand the client better. A second important reason for listening fully to the story of the referral source is that on many occasions I have found that a person who refers a client to me has real issues of her own which have arisen as a result of trying to help the client. Whenever I have ignored what the referral person wished to tell me, I have ignored her needs, and have failed to listen to the issues which she needed to resolve for herself.

The preamble

The initial meeting with a client is extremely important. The client's first impressions of the counsellor will influence her willingness to share openly. First impressions can be enduring and even if they aren't, they are likely to influence the early part of the relationship. It is therefore very important that the climate of the relationship is established right from the beginning. What I do, as I move towards the client to greet her, in some ways affects her feelings towards me, and her confidence in me. For me, it's important that each person I meet feels valued and at ease with me. I like to be seen as an ordinary person, somebody who is not intimidating, neither expert nor inferior, but friendly, open and informal. You will have your own style, of course, and it will quite probably be very different from mine. However, be aware of your style. Make sure that you come over as warm and genuine. Be yourself.

As you greet the client you will, if you are aware, pick up a lot of information from her. Notice the way she is sitting or standing. Her non-verbal behaviour will tell you something about the way she feels. Look at the clothes she is wearing, and how they are worn. By doing this you will learn something about how she sees herself, and how she wants to be seen. You may also learn something about her financial situation. Don't jump to unverified conclusions, but use the information gleaned from your first meeting, so that you can gradually build up a picture of the client's world and of her view of that world.

When I meet a client for the first time, I introduce myself and usually chat to her as we walk to my counselling room. This helps her to feel at ease. When I meet her prior to subsequent interviews I am generally less chatty, and often silent. This enables the client to stay with any troubling thoughts rather than to be taken away from them. Be aware that as a client leaves the waiting room and walks to your consulting room, she may well be putting her thoughts together, and may be experiencing the beginnings of heavy emotion as she gets nearer to the issues that she wants to discuss. If she is doing that, then it isn't helpful to be talking about trivia. It's better to be silent.

Notice that I have differentiated between the first and subsequent sessions. I try to help the client to feel very much at ease during the first session, and am happy to sacrifice a few minutes of time during that meeting to allow the client to feel comfortable with me, and with the room that I work in. I allow the client to sit down, to look around, and maybe to comment on my plants or some other aspect of my room or the agency. We may even talk about some other casual topic like how she travelled to the agency, and what the traffic was like, or I may share something of myself and my day with her. As a result we start to establish a relationship before moving forwards into working on issues.

So far, we have been discussing the preamble to the counselling session. The preamble really is important in helping to establish the counselling relationship so that the client feels at ease. It also helps the counsellor to check out and adjust some of her initial ideas about the client.

Getting started

After the initial settling-in period described above, I usually start the working part of the session by asking the client how she feels emotionally, *right now.* This enables the client to get in touch with her own anxiety or tension about coming for counselling. By getting in touch with these feelings, a change usually occurs, and this makes it easier for the client to move on to talking about the issues troubling her.

Sometimes a client will come with a "shopping list" of things which she wishes to talk about, and may even produce lengthy hand-written notes. If a client has done this I try to make her feel that what she has done is useful and valuable preparation. However, I avoid getting trapped into working through the shopping list item by item, but instead use the list to generate energy in the client. For example, I might say, "This list is really important.

When you think about it, what do you think about first?". Thus the client finds a starting point from which she can proceed naturally, in whatever direction her energy takes her. More often than not the shopping list will become irrelevant as more important underlying issues emerge.

Unfortunately clients often perceive counsellors as "experts", with almost magical skills, who are capable of using clever psychological techniques to solve other people's problems. Consequently, there may need to be a re-education process, where you, the counsellor, spell out to the client exactly how you *do* see yourself. It may be necessary for you to say to the client, "Look, I don't see myself as an expert who can solve your problems for you. In fact, I believe that you will always know and understand yourself better than I will know and understand you. However, I hope that in this session you and I together can explore what's troubling you so that you can make some progress towards feeling more comfortable". Alternatively, you might say something like, "It would be great if I were a magician who could wave a wand over you to solve your problems. I can't do that, but I can offer you the opportunity to come here and explore your problems with me in a safe and confidential setting. Hopefully, by doing that, you will start to feel more comfortable".

Active listening

During the early parts of a session, as the client starts to talk about her issues, the counsellor is able to make use of minimal responses, and to reflect content and feelings. By doing this the client is encouraged to disclose what is troubling her, in her own way and at her own pace, and without unnecessary intrusion into that process by the counsellor. Consequently the client's story unfolds and the relationship between client and counsellor develops as the client feels valued by the counsellor's active listening.

In the early stages of counselling it is common for clients to be unable to recognize and talk about their emotional feelings. Clients often want to talk about things "out there" rather than inside themselves. They want to talk about other people's behaviour, and about other people's fears. They want to focus on what happened in the past rather than on the present, and to focus on events, instead of on their own inner feelings. It is useful to encourage a client, in this situation, to focus on her inner feelings and thoughts, as they are, in the present, if she will. However, it is also important not to pressure her, but to allow her to move at her own pace. At first, allow your client to talk about the "out there" things, if it is too painful for her to focus on her own inner processes. With time, as she deals with the "out there" problems, and with the "out there" situations, she is likely to move slowly towards recognizing and talking about her own feelings from the past. Past feelings

will not be so threatening to her as present feelings. Later in the counselling process, she will move towards experiencing her present feelings. Move *slowly* towards helping the client to experience her own thoughts and feelings in the present. It is important to do this sensitively because the client needs to be able to gradually approach the painful parts of her life, rather than to be pushed too quickly, and then to run away from looking at the issues that are troubling her. The counsellor who pushes too hard, too early does the client a disservice, because the client will either close the lid on her Pandora's box of uncomfortable feelings and thoughts, or will not come back to another counselling session.

During the active listening phase, whilst keeping a check on her own inner experiences, the counsellor needs to focus her energy by concentrating as totally as she is able on what is happening inside the counselling room. In particular she needs to fully attend to the client, to concentrate on listening to and observing the client, and to sense what the client is experiencing. This is not always easy. For example, after a night on duty working for a crisis counselling agency, sometimes my attention has wandered when working with a client during the next day. Rather than trying to cover up my lapse of attention, I've stopped and said "Look, I really want to give you my full attention, and my attention wandered just then. I need to tell you that I was out during the night last night attending to a crisis. I'm feeling very tired today but I am going to put all the remaining energy I have into working with you. Please will you repeat what you have just said?". By being open and honest, I've been able to re-establish a close relationship with the client and have been able to muster the additional energy to carry on an effective counselling session. Of course it is not ideal to be counselling when over-tired, but we don't live in an ideal word, and there will always be times when the counsellor makes the mistake of over-extending herself (see Chapter 27 on the subject of burnout).

Problem identification and clarification

At times, the counsellor will need to draw together the important parts of what the client has said, and to help the client to focus more clearly by summarizing these. As the client's trust develops, the counsellor will be able to ask appropriate questions where necessary, in order to help the client move forwards and identify her most pressing problem.

Facilitating attitude change

The skills of reframing, confrontation and challenging self-destructive beliefs can now be used, if appropriate, to encourage the client to choose more constructive attitudes and beliefs.

Exploring options and facilitating action

The counsellor may now be able to assist the client to move forwards into exploring options, resolving dilemmas and planning for action. However, it is important to ensure that the client does not feel pressured. Remember, as described in Chapters 14 and 15, to put energy into the raising of awareness rather than into pushing for choice or action. To prematurely encourage a client to make a choice will pressure her and will make it harder for her to reach a decision. If the client is not ready to make a choice, she must be allowed to feel that it is OK to be unable to make a decision, and to feel that it is OK for her to remain stuck for the present.

Termination

A good way to terminate a counselling session is to summarize the important awarenesses which have emerged during the session. Don't attempt to summarize everything that was covered in the session, as that is unnecessary and unhelpful. Just pick out what was important. Imagine that at the start of the session the client brought into the room an awkward bundle of thoughts and feelings. She dropped the bundle on to the floor and started to examine the contents one at a time. After examining each item, she retained some, threw some away and exchanged others. After that it was time to help her tie up the bundle into a neater, more manageable package. The idea of the summary is to help her do this. To see the whole package as it is now, and to tie up those loose ends that can be tied up right now.

Of course it isn't always possible to neatly tie up the package. Sometimes the client will be left in a very uncomfortable space, either feeling stuck, or fairly unhappy, or distressed about what she has discovered. New counsellors usually want clients to leave sessions feeling happy. It is important to remember that often it is useful for a client to be able to spend time mulling over what has been discussed in the counselling session. She can then process it on her own before coming back again if she needs to. Even so, it can be distressing to a new counsellor to find a client waiting for her in the waiting room before a session, looking composed, and then leaving the session with tears in her eyes. This will inevitably happen at times. Frequently, in a counselling session, the client moves into areas which she previously had not been prepared to openly explore. She allows herself to feel the pain of experiencing emotions that had been suppressed, and she leaves the counselling session exhausted and sad. However, allowing the client to do this is highly therapeutic and the positive results of this process will be seen when the client returns for a subsequent session.

The process of a counselling session described in this chapter gives an overview of the process which might occur in a counselling session. However,

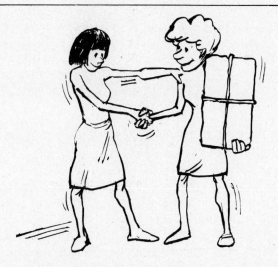

as a counsellor, do not attempt to follow this process, but rather let it emerge naturally. Do as described in Chapter 2: allow the client to go at her own pace, in her own direction, and to feel as though she is going on a journey with you, the counsellor, walking alongside. If you do this, the counselling process will occur naturally, smoothly and without great effort on your part. Most importantly, the client will be undergoing a process of growth which will inevitably enable her to lead a more fulfilling and less painful life.

18 The immediacy of the counselling experience

I am sure that you know people who are in the habit of continually complaining about their life situations, and who like to talk at length about the injustices of the world. They talk about things which are "out there" and which are apparently out of their control and are the responsibility of others. Rather than saying "What can I do to change this situation?" they use statements with words in them like "They should . . .", and "They ought . . .", and "It's disgraceful that they don't . . . ". Such people often go over the same ground again and again. This is really inevitable because no-one can change a situation which is not within his own sphere of control.

Do you ever behave like the people I've just described? Do you ever grumble, moan and complain about "out there" things, things that are apparently other people's responsibility rather than yours? I do.

Notice how we started talking about other "people who complain" in this chapter and are now looking at ourselves. My guess is that you were more comfortable when the discussion was about others than you were when owning your own ability to grumble and complain. It's usually easier for us to distance ourselves from our own dysfunctional behaviour and to blame others for our problems. Unfortunately if I complain about things that other people are doing or not doing, or about external events or situations, then I am likely to get stuck in a rut of complaining, and to feel frustrated because I am powerless to bring about change. Conversely, if I focus on what I myself am doing, and on what is happening inside me, then I can, if I choose, take action to change what I am doing, or I can change my thinking so that I am better able to accept what is happening.

Similar logic to that just discussed applies to the present when compared with the past and future. I have no control over past events, they have already happened and I can't change them. Similarly, I have limited control over future events, they have not happened yet and I cannot be sure what the future will bring. Inappropriately focusing on the past and future is likely to lead me into unending philosophizing, complaining, and worrying, whereas focusing on the present allows me to make sensible choices for my own satisfaction.

The preceding discussion is not meant to imply that it is useless in a counselling session for the client to talk about what other people are doing, to talk about situations beyond his control, or to talk about past or future events, but it does mean that there is no point whatever in the client doing this unless he also focuses on what is happening inside him, at the present time, when he thinks about these situations or events. The focus in counselling needs to be on what is happening within the client at the moment in question, in the *here and now*, if the intervention is to be optimally therapeutic.

Let us imagine a situation where a client is really angry about the way his father treated him when he was a young child. He could talk about this past relationship time and again and make little progress. However, if the counsellor brings the focus on to what is happening within the client at the time when he talks about the past, then progress will be made. The counsellor might then tap into anger, resentment and bitterness which is present right now. As the counsellor listens to descriptions of past experiences, it is appropriate for him to ask the client how he feels as he talks about them. The counsellor might say, "Tell me how you feel emotionally *right now*, as you talk about those past events." By doing this, the counsellor brings the focus into the present, and brings current emotional feelings which are associated with the past traumas into the client's awareness. The client is then able to fully experience those feelings and deal with them appropriately. It is only by fully experiencing these emotional feelings that the client will be able, either to reduce or rid himself of them, or to discover ways of dealing with them constructively. One way of bringing the client's focus into the present is to watch his non-verbal behaviour and to tell him what you notice, or alternatively to ask a question about what he is experiencing emotionally. For example, the client's eyes may become watery as he recounts some past event. Sensitively interrupting with the words "I notice the tears starting to form in your eyes" or "Tell me what you are experiencing emotionally right now" is very likely to bring the client more fully in touch with his present internal experiences. Give your client permission to take time, to stay with his feelings, and to experience them. In that way he is allowed to cry if he is hurting, is allowed to express his anger if he is angry, and is allowed to own whatever other emotion may be within him, and so to move forwards into a more comfortable space.

Gradually the client will learn to allow himself to experience his feelings rather than to deny them. This learning, in the counselling situation, will hopefully extend into the client's daily life and enable him to be more responsive to his feelings generally. Thus he will be enabled to deal with his feelings as they arise rather than letting them build up to an intolerable level.

A common cause of client distress is an inability to properly and appropriately express "negative" feelings towards others. For many people, for example, the expression of anger is repressed from childhood. Whenever small children get angry their parents tend to say "Don't you behave in that angry way. Don't throw a tantrum". As a result the child learns, incorrectly, that it isn't appropriate to express anger towards others even when an angry reaction is justified. Unfortunately blocked anger leads to depression. What is worse, if we don't tell other people how we feel about them, then we prevent ourselves having fully functioning, open, and genuine, relationships with them. It is important to bring issues out into the open and discuss them, even if that is painful, rather than suppressing feelings and pretending that they don't exist. The immediacy of the counselling relationship can be used to demonstrate how feelings can be shared in a constructive way which enhances rather than damages the relationship.

In the immediacy of the counselling situation there is a real-life relationship between the client and counsellor. A skilled counsellor will naturally model adaptive and constructive ways of relating, and will also help the client to explore feelings which are generated by the counselling relationship. By learning to explore these feelings and bring them into the open, the client learns appropriate ways in which to deal with the feelings which are generated by his relationships with others, and hence is likely to improve the quality of his relationships generally.

Imagine that by carefully observing the non-verbal behaviour of a client, a counsellor suspects that the client is angry with him. The counsellor may have noticed, for example, an angry look flash across the client's face. It is easy to misinterpret non-verbal behaviour and so it's important for the counsellor to check out whether in fact it was an angry look. The counsellor might say, "I've got the impression that you looked angry then", and as a result the client may then become aware of his anger and may be willing to explore it more fully. In this way the client's feelings are brought out into the open and the counsellor can respond appropriately and genuinely so that his relationship with the client is more complete.

If the counsellor is to be genuine in his relationship with the client, then he will need to share his own emotions about the relationship with him when this is appropriate. It can be useful for a client to be made aware of the counsellor's emotional responses particularly when these relate to the relationship between client and counsellor. If the counsellor is annoyed by the client's behaviour towards him, he needs to say so, so that the client can learn how his behaviour is perceived. In this way the client can, if he chooses, change. Changing may significantly affect his life as it may be that the way in which he annoys the counsellor is similar to the way in which he annoys other people in his life generally. Unfortunately, most people are too polite to give useful feedback to friends, even when their friends exhibit extremely destructive and maladaptive behaviours.

As an example of feedback, a counsellor may need to say to a client, "I feel irritated when you interrupt". By doing this, the client may discover that his tendency to interrupt is irritating, and he can if he wishes change that behaviour. Obviously, such feedback needs to be given in a way which is non-threatening and acceptable for the client. When you give feedback, avoid starting your sentence with the word "you" but instead use "I". A typical feedback statement would have the following structure. " I feel . . . when . . . " By starting with the words "I feel", the counsellor is owning and sharing his own feelings and this makes it easier for the client to hear what is being said, and makes it less likely that he will feel attacked and become defensive.

Notice again the example given: "I feel irritated when you interrupt me". The statement after the word "when" is a concrete statement of fact and not an interpretation. To say, for example, "I feel irritated when you interrupt me because you don't want to listen to what I'm saying" would involve an interpretation of the client's behaviour which might be incorrect. Be careful not to include interpretations in feedback statements. The following are some examples of appropriate and inappropriate feedback statements. See if you can decide which are appropriate and which are not, and then check your decision by reading the comments at the end of this chapter.

Examples of appropriate and inappropriate feedback statements

1. You keep coming late to appointments because you don't think it's worthwhile to come to counselling.
2. I am puzzled when I notice that you continually come late for appointments.
3. You have put a barrier between us because you dislike me.
4. You are treating me like a father and I'm not your father.
5. I am uncomfortable because to me it feels as though you are relating to me like a son relates to his father.
6. Right now I have a shut-out feeling, as though there is a closed door between us.

From these examples and the comments provided at the end of the chapter, you will have noticed that appropriate feedback involves the counsellor owning his own feelings in the relationship and sharing these together with a concrete statement of fact. Inappropriate feedback accuses, blames or interprets the client's behaviour and generally starts with the word "you".

Note that it is sometimes useful to teach clients how to use "I" statements themselves, instead of "you" statements. Teach them using the "I feel . . . when . . . " structure, as this is easy to understand. Stress the importance of making concrete factual statements and of not making interpretations.

Appropriately given feedback will leave a client feeling cared for and valued. Remember that a counsellor does not need to like a client's behaviour to be accepting of the client. It is not inconsistent to say, "I don't like it when you do that" and also to say, "I really care about you a great deal and accept you the way you are". I can accept someone the way he is without liking his behaviour. At a deeper level, I can love someone without liking all of his behaviour.

The immediacy of the counselling relationship often raises questions regarding what psychoanalysts call *transference* and *counter-transference*. Transference occurs when a client behaves toward a counsellor as though the counsellor were a significant person from the client's past, usually the client's father. Naturally, it is quite possible for the counsellor to inadvertently fall into playing the role in which the client sees him. That is, if the client relates to the counsellor as though the counsellor were his father, the counsellor might start feeling and behaving like a father. Such behaviour is called counter-transference. It is inevitable that transference and counter-transference will occur at times in the counselling relationship but, provided that this is recognized, brought into the open and discussed, it is not a problem. It would, however, be a problem if it were not brought out into the open, as it is not useful for the client to treat the counsellor as though he were someone from the past.

It may be that in some ways the counsellor is like the client's father, but in other ways he is not, and it is important for the counsellor to make the distinction clear. This enables a genuine relationship between client and counsellor to occur rather than one which is coloured totally by the client's past experiences with a significant other. When the counsellor realizes that transference may be occurring, he might say "I feel as though you are relating to me rather like a son relates to his father".

Where counter-transference is occurring, the relevant counsellor statement might be "Right now I feel rather like a father to you". The counsellor needs to point out caringly that he is not the client's father or any other significant person from the client's past, and that he is himself: unique and different.

Through the immediacy of the counselling relationship the client may learn something about his tendency to project characteristics of significant others from his past on to the people he relates to and so may be able to recognize when inappropriate projection on to others is damaging his relationships. Whenever you notice what is happening in the relationship between you and your client, bring it into the open. If you sense that something unusual, different or important is happening in the relationship between yourself and your client, then tell him what you are observing, so that it is fully discussed and explored. By exploring such material the client is able to learn more about himself, to realize what he does in relationships, and to become more conscious of his internal emotional experiences and thoughts. As a result, he is able to move forwards and to develop more fully as a person.

New counsellors are troubled at times by a client's apparent lack of co-operation with the therapeutic process. This is called "resistance". A good example of resistance is provided by clients who come late for appointments or who miss appointments repeatedly. Of course, there may be good reasons for a client doing such things. It is well to be aware, though, that often the explanations given may be more in the nature of rationalizations or excuses than the real reason why the behaviour is occurring. For example, a client may be finding counselling very threatening and worrying, and may, for subconscious reasons, be postponing his involvement. It is important for the client to realize what is happening so that the real issue is addressed, and the client's fear is dealt with. Once again, what the counsellor needs to do is to verbalize what he is noticing.

Let me give you another interesting example of resistance. As a trainer of counsellors, I have noticed that often trainee counsellors have come to supervision sessions and have said to me, "Look I haven't been able to make the video tape that I promised to make last week, of a counselling session of mine", then they have told me some reason why it was quite impossible for them to make the video tape. "Oh, I couldn't find a blank cassette", or "The machine jammed when I put the cassette in", or "I put the cassette in and unfortunately I pushed the wrong button and it didn't record", or "Unfortunately somebody else borrowed the video before I did as I had forgotten to book it". Now of course, all of those "excuses" were valid. They were all genuine. The trainee counsellor was at no time lying but was being genuine and honest. However, resistance was usually discovered when I said something like this: "I notice that for three weeks in a row you have failed to produce a video, and yet you appear to have had perfectly good reasons. I am puzzled by this because you seem to be an intelligent and competent person". This statement has enabled the trainee to explore more fully what was happening, and it has usually been discovered that it was threatening for the trainee to produce a video, and yes, if he had made a little more effort, it would have been possible to have produced the recording. It has never been necessary for me to say "You must produce a video next week"; rather, just drawing attention to what I have observed has been sufficient to overcome the trainee's resistance. Similarly, in the counselling process with clients, if you notice that a client is repeatedly late, or has missed several appointments in a row, draw the client's attention to what has happened. It may be necessary to say "Yes, I have heard your reasons and I understand and believe them but I am still left wondering whether at some other level something else is happening. I am puzzled that so often you should be late".

Resistance can, of course, take many forms. Sometimes resistance blocks a client from exploring a particularly painful area in his life, and as a counsellor you may feel frustrated by such avoidance. It is however, in my opinion, important to go with the resistance rather than trying to burst through it. There are differences of opinion here, however, as some counsellors believe that actually smashing through the resistance is the way to go. I prefer the opposite approach, probably because I have an interest in Gestalt therapy. I go with the resistance by drawing the client's attention to what is happening. I might say to a client, "I've noticed that you find it far too painful to discuss that particular area of your life so let's leave it alone altogether, let's just put it away, and not deal with it". The client is then able to fully experience his avoidance and usually something important will emerge spontaneously. If it does not then I would ask the client what he was currently experiencing. As a result the client would be brought in touch with what it feels like to avoid exploring a painful area of his life and consequently might decide how to deal with his avoidance. Alternatively he might say, "I'm not prepared to explore that really painful area of my life. To do so would be like opening up Pandora's box. It's far too scary for me". He has a right to make that choice and to leave Pandora's box closed. If that is what he chooses I respect his wishes.

In this chapter we have dealt with the ways in which the immediacy of the counselling relationship can be used to:

1. help the client to focus on his own behaviour, inner feelings and thoughts, in the present, rather than focusing on past behaviours, or on the behaviour of others over which he has no control;

2. help the client to learn to own and deal with his emotional feelings as they arise. This includes owning and dealing with so-called "negative" feelings towards others;

3. give the client acceptable feedback with regard to inappropriate behaviours which cause annoyance to the counsellor and may annoy others;

4. help the client to recognize and deal with his human tendency to project the characteristics of significant persons from his past onto others;

5. help the client to deal with his own resistance.

An effective counsellor will verbalize his observations of what is occurring in the immediacy of the counselling relationship so that client growth is promoted. Hopefully, what is learnt from the counselling experience will be carried into the client's everyday life.

Comments on examples of appropriate and inappropriate feedback statements

1. INAPPROPRIATE FEEDBACK. The statement is threatening as it starts with the word "you". The words "because you don't think it's worthwhile to come to counselling" are an unverified interpretation of the client's behaviour.

2. APPROPRIATE FEEDBACK. The counsellor starts with an "I" statement which describes how he feels: "I am puzzled". He then gives a concrete statement of what he has observed: "You continually come late for appointments". The counsellor does not attempt to interpret the client's behaviour, but merely states what he observes.

3. INAPPROPRIATE FEEDBACK. The statement is inappropriate because it consists of a "you" statement which could make the client feel attacked. Moreover, the counsellor is interpreting the client's behaviour. His statement, "You dislike me" is guesswork and could well be wrong.

4. INAPPROPRIATE FEEDBACK. An inappropriate statement starting with "you" which could be received by the client as a put down.

5. APPROPRIATE FEEDBACK. This statement appropriately starts with the counsellor saying how he feels: "I am uncomfortable". Instead of accusing his client by using a "you" statement, the counsellor goes on to explain how the relationship feels for him. Compare this statement with Example 4. It is very different.

6. APPROPRIATE FEEDBACK. Notice how in this statement the counsellor describes how he feels rather than blaming the client for putting up a barrier. Compare this statement with Example 3.

19 The human personality as it emerges in the counselling experience

It is blatantly obvious that the human personality is incredibly complex. In order to help us understand the ways in which people behave, it is useful to describe human personality in terms of easily understandable models. Any model which we use is certain to be a gross over-simplification, but even so it may help us to understand better what happens in ourselves and in our clients. I think that a good model for human personality is the iceberg. Icebergs float so that most of the iceberg is below the water-line and cannot be seen. Human beings are a bit like that. As you get to know a person, you will see parts of her personality. You will see those parts that are, metaphorically speaking, above the water-line. There are other parts of that person's personality too, but you do not see these as they are submerged below the water-line. Even the person herself will not be fully aware of all those parts of herself which are below the water-line. Icebergs have a tendency to roll over from time to time and as they roll over, some parts of the iceberg that had previously been submerged come into sight. From time to time, parts of a person's personality that were hidden come unexpectedly into view, rather like those parts of the iceberg that show when it rolls over. Sometimes it is other people who are surprised by what they see when this happens, and sometimes the person herself gets a surprise too.

An interesting characteristic of human personality is the existence of polarities or opposites. The most commonly talked-about polarities are "love" and "hate". How often have you heard someone talk about a love/hate relationship? As you are probably aware from your own experience the love-hate relationship really does exist. If I have a strong capacity for loving, then it is certain that I also have the potential to hate. I may of course deny my capacity to hate. Just imagine the iceberg with the word "love" sitting on the top, out in the open for everyone to see, and the word "hate" right down below the sea, and hidden from view. The danger exists that one day the iceberg will roll over and the "hate" side will be all that will be seen. Time and time again we see a relationship where a couple falls in love, and then the relationship breaks up, and the love that was there is replaced, not by something neutral, but by hate.

Hostility and acceptance are another set of polarities. Sometimes if I'm feeling very angry with somebody, my hostility prevents me from forgiving and accepting them. It seems as though forgiveness and acceptance are on the opposite side of the iceberg to anger and hostility. If the iceberg rolls around so that my anger is uppermost, then forgiveness is buried beneath the sea. However, it's only by fully accepting my anger, by experiencing it totally, and by allowing it to surface fully, that I am able to make the iceberg roll over again and reveal forgiveness.

It's important for me to recognize that opposites exist within me, because if I want to strengthen a particular quality, I need to accept and deal with its opposite. I'm capable of loving and hating. I'm capable of anger and I'm capable of being forgiving. I'm capable of being tolerant and capable of being intolerant. I'm capable of being generous and miserly, I'm capable of being optimistic and of being pessimistic, of being fun-loving and of being a kill-joy, of being light-hearted and of being serious, of being religious and of having doubts about my religious values and beliefs. In order to feel integrated and comfortable within myself, I need to accept all the parts of me, and not just those parts that are socially acceptable and consistent with my being a "nice" person.

Clients often come to counselling because they are unable to accept parts of themselves. It seems as if parts of themselves have become submerged beneath the sea, never to be seen, and never to be owned. The submerged parts are continually wanting to surface, and there is an inner struggle to prevent the iceberg from rolling over. Naturally clients feel great discomfort when they try to keep parts of themselves submerged and try to deny parts of themselves that really want to be expressed.

A common example of client distress caused by suppressing a part of self is the depression caused by repressed anger. Time and again with depressed clients, I find that they are unable to express their anger. Often, when I suggest to them that maybe they feel angry with the person who has wronged them, I'll be met with a denial. "No I'm not angry, I'm just sad," they will say. Gradually, however, as the counselling relationship builds up, they will begin to express themselves more fully. After a counselling session or two, the depression will start to lift, and anger will emerge. At first the anger will be barely expressed and will be described in very mild terms, but gradually it will build up. The more this happens, the more the depression recedes.

As explained in Chapter 18, many of us are taught from childhood to deny what our parents, teachers and other significant persons regard as negative emotions. It is almost inevitable that parents will put anger into this category and tell their children not to be angry but to calm down. As a result, most children learn to think of anger as a negative emotion and start to disown it, saying "No, I'm not really angry" when they are really very angry indeed.

Paradoxically, if I fully accept and own my anger, then I can deal with it constructively. Often it will disappear spontaneously and in its place I will experience a more comfortable emotion. It is important for me, however, to recognize that I have a potential for anger and to allow that potential to exist rather than suppressing it. Of course, in saying this, I recognize that we are all unique and different. There are people in the world whose anger is a danger to themselves and others. For them, continually letting their anger out is not constructive, but rather maladaptive behaviour. See Chapter 20 for ideas on how to deal with angry clients.

I've devoted this chapter to the polarities model because I have found this model useful for helping clients to feel OK about accepting and owning what they initially believe are undesirable or negative qualities or emotions. I tell my clients that for every so-called positive or desirable emotion or quality, normal human beings also have the opposite emotion or quality. This is normal and therefore OK. Such thinking frees clients to deal with all their emotions, personal qualities, traits and attributes. They are then able to strengthen those parts of themselves which they would like to strengthen, and can grow as people accordingly.

PART IV
Some specialized counselling areas

This section of the book deals with angry, suicidal and grieving clients. It is inevitable that before long a new counsellor will find that some clients who come to see him will fall into these categories. It is important to know your own limitations as a counsellor and to refer such clients to experienced and skilled therapists, after consultation with your supervisor, whenever appropriate. However, the problems of anger, suicide, and grief are so common that it is important for new counsellors to have an understanding of useful ways in which to work with such clients.

20   The angry client

Counsellors frequently have to deal with angry clients. Bottled-up anger can be very destructive and also very dangerous because it may break out at some time or other and the client may do injury or damage to another person. Many counsellors, in the early stages of their counselling careers, become quite frightened when clients exhibit even moderate levels of anger. This chapter has been included to provide new counsellors with some practical ideas about how to deal with angry clients in cases where it is not considered necessary to refer them to a more experienced therapist.

An angry client needs to be able to dissipate his anger if he is to feel better. There are two different and complementary ways of helping him to do this. One way is to encourage the client to verbally release his anger in the safety of the counselling environment, and the other is to teach the client relaxation. Also, once the client's initial anger level has been reduced, he can be taught constructive ways to control his anger in the future.

A client can be allowed to verbally release his anger in the counselling room provided that he is neither dangerous nor violent. Whenever an inexperienced counsellor suspects a client of having a potential for violence, the counsellor should refer the client to a suitably qualified and experienced therapist.

When a client starts to express his anger use the normal reflective methods if you wish, but if his level of anger starts to rise then it's sensible for you, the counsellor, to take control and ensure that the anger is directed away from yourself. As a counsellor do not allow the client's anger to rise significantly while he is talking directly to you, or you may end up feeling tense yourself. Instead, protect yourself by using a method borrowed from Gestalt Therapy (for an explanation of Gestalt Therapy see Polster and Polster, 1974). The method is as follows:

Start by asking the client who he is most angry with. Next, place an empty chair facing the client and a metre or more away from him. Tell the client to imagine that sitting in the empty chair is the person who is the target of his anger. Say to the client something like, "I don't want to be the recipient of your anger, and so I don't want you to tell me how angry you are, rather I'd like you to talk to the imaginary person who is sitting in that empty chair, about your angry feelings towards him". Preferably you should now stand beside your client and join him in facing the empty chair. You can then "coach" the client in his expression of anger towards the imagined person.

For example, if the client starts saying "Well actually I'm very angry with Fred, because Fred has consistently offended me with his behaviour," then, as counsellor, you can say yourself, "*I'm* very angry with you Fred, because you've consistently behaved badly". The client will then pick up the way in which he is expected to address the imagined person on the empty chair instead of talking to you, and he can then be encouraged to express his anger openly and fully. This method is useful for the client as it enables him to verbalize his anger, and avoids a situation where the counsellor becomes the recipient of the anger, because the counsellor is standing beside the client and joining with him. If this method appeals to you, then after completion of your basic counsellor training, you may wish to train as a Gestalt Therapist and learn other powerful techniques for enabling clients to release their anger.

Remember that some clients have great difficulty in controlling inappropriately high levels of anger. Among these people are the wife, husband and child bashers. They must be referred to skilled psychotherapists and are not suitable clients for a new counsellor.

As well as enabling the client to verbally release his anger in the way described previously, it may be useful to teach the client relaxation or meditation in order to reduce his emotional level. There are many different ways of teaching both relaxation and meditation. The following relaxation exercise is one that I use. If you wish to use it, you can read the following instructions to your client using a quiet, slow, monotonous tone of voice. Pause between each statement for a few seconds.

Relaxation exercise

Lie on the floor with your head on a cushion, your hands beside you, and your legs straight.

Move around until you feel comfortable.

Close your eyes.

You will probably enjoy this exercise and find it pleasurable, but if at any time you are feeling uncomfortable and want to stop you may either choose to lie quietly and ignore my voice, or you may speak up and tell me that you want to discontinue the exercise.

Notice where your body touches the floor.

Move yourself so that you are more comfortable.

Be aware of your whole body from head to toe and stretch any part of you that is uncomfortable.

Let your body press down on the floor.

Notice the floor pressing up on you.

It's a good feeling.

You are in contact with the ground and the ground is in contact with you.
Notice your breathing.
Allow yourself to breathe comfortably and naturally.

(Longer pause)

We are going to go through a series of exercises during which you will relax
  various parts of your body starting from the tip of your toes and
  finishing at the top of your head.
For each set of muscles, I will suggest that you tighten those muscles whilst
  breathing in deeply, and then relax them as you breathe out.
Whenever you remember, say to yourself the word "relax" as you breathe out.
In between relaxing each set of muscles, focus on your breathing again.
Breathe naturally and say "relax" silently to yourself as you breathe out each
  time. By doing this you will become aware of nothing but your
  breathing and will gradually become more relaxed. If any intruding
  thoughts come into your mind, don't worry, just return to focusing on
  your breathing again.
Notice your breathing now.
Each time you breathe out say "relax" silently to yourself.

(NOTE TO COUNSELLOR: Observe the client's body, and notice his breathing.
When he breathes out each time say the word "relax" quietly. Do this a few
times so that the client remembers to do it himself.)

Notice your body. If any parts of it are uncomfortable, stretch or move so
  that you are more comfortable.
Focus on your breathing.
When you are ready, I will ask you, as you breathe in, to take a slow deep
  breath and as you do this to clench your toes tightly and tighten up the
  muscles in your feet.

(COUNSELLOR: choose the time)

Breathe in deeply and tighten up the muscles in your feet.
Hold your breath and keep the muscles in your feet tight for a few seconds.
Breathe out heavily and release the tension in your feet.
Continue breathing naturally and say "relax" to yourself each time you
  breathe out.

(Wait for a while as the client continues to breath naturally)

Now tense your thigh and calf muscles as you breathe in deeply.
Hold your breath and keep your muscles tense.

Relax as you breathe out.
Breathe naturally and feel relaxed.

(pause a while)

Tense the muscles in your buttocks as you breathe in deeply.
Hold your breath and keep your muscles tensed.
Now breathe out and relax.
Breathe naturally and notice a feeling of relaxation flowing up your body
from your feet to your buttocks.

(pause a while)

Tense the muscles in your abdomen as you breathe in deeply.
Hold your breath.
Relax.
Notice your breathing.

(pause a while)

Clench your fists as you breathe in.
Hold.
Relax.

(pause a while)

Now tense the muscles in your arms and stretch your fingers out as you
breathe in.
Hold.
Relax.
Notice a relaxed feeling flow up from your feet through your calves, thighs,
abdomen, hands, arms and chest.
Let your body sink into the floor and feel supported by the floor.
Breathe naturally.

(pause)

Tighten your shoulder and neck muscles as you breathe in.
Hold.
Relax.

(pause)

Clench your teeth, screw up your face, close your eyes tightly, and feel your
    scalp tighten as you breathe in.
Hold.
Relax.

(pause)

Breathe naturally and notice the relaxed feeling moving up and
    encompassing your whole body.
Be aware of your breathing. Each time you breathe out feel yourself
    becoming more relaxed.

(Long pause)

Soon it will be time to start getting in touch with your surroundings again.
    When you do this, allow yourself to feel good, to be wide awake and
    alert.

(pause)

Notice the floor. Move your fingers and feel it.
Wriggle slightly and when you are ready open your eyes.
Lie where you are and look around. Allow yourself to take in what you see, to
    feel good, and to be awake and alert.
When you are ready, roll over sideways and support yourself with one arm in
    a half-sitting position.
Sit up when the time is right for you.

The above relaxation exercise can be taught to a client in a counselling
session, and he can then be encouraged to practise it regularly in his own
time. However, warn your client about the dangers of being too relaxed. It is
not, for example, advisable to drive a car in a very relaxed state. A certain
amount of tension is useful so that the client's reactions to danger are fast.
Therefore, do not go through the relaxation exercise with your client
immediately before he is due to drive away!
    Once a client has learnt to relax by muscle tensing and relaxing he will
find it easier to relax when standing up and in a tense situation. Teach him
to take a few deep breaths and each time he breathes in to tighten up his
muscles and then relax as he breathes out. With practice he will probably
find that he will be able to let himself relax as he breathes out naturally. If
you wish to learn more about progressive relaxation training, read Bernstein
and Borkovec (1973).

Once the client's initially high anger level has started to subside, the next stage is to teach him how to deal with his anger in the future. Give your client a copy of the chart shown in Figure 7 and discuss it with him.

Although the chart is fairly self-explanatory, it is useful to work through it step by step. The first step is for the client to learn to recognize physiological cues. When I start to get angry, things happen to my body. I might notice that my heart rate increases and that I breathe more rapidly. I might start to sweat, my muscles might tighten up, or I might have an uncomfortable feeling in my stomach. Some people freeze on the spot and feel their hair standing on end. We are all different and so each individual needs to identify for himself what happens to him physiologically when he starts to get angry. Once a client has learnt to recognize the physiological symptoms that occur as his anger starts to rise, he can use them as cues for appropriate action. He is then able to make a choice, either to allow an angry outburst to occur, or to stop and react differently. At times it may be better to allow controlled angry outbursts to occur, rather than to bottle up the emotion. Clearly, uncontrolled angry outbursts are dangerous, but letting off steam by continually having small outbursts does enable anger to be dissipated. Unfortunately, people who continually behave angrily are certain to damage their relationships with others.

The alternative to having an angry outburst is for the client to recognize the physiological cues that indicate a rise in anger and immediately to say "STOP" silently to himself. This is called thought-stopping. I knew a counsellor once who used to teach thought-stopping by getting his client to shut his eyes and imagine a scene that would make him angry. When the client was concentrating on that scene the counsellor would slam a book down on the desk and shout "STOP". The sudden impact would stop the client in his tracks. In fact, it would give the client such a fright that I do not use this method myself for fear of unpleasant consequences! However, this method did demonstrate effectively to the client that he could stop his thoughts instantly, and change their direction if he chose to do so.

Once a client has stopped letting his thoughts hook him into an angry outburst, he can make the choice to step back from the situation, to mentally move back 10 metres so that he is, in effect, looking at himself and his situation from a distant vantage point. He can then, if he chooses, take a few deep slow breaths and allow the muscles in his body to relax in the way that he has been taught in the muscle relaxation exercise. As he takes those few deep slow breaths, each time he breathes out he can say silently to himself, "relax", and allow his body to relax.

The next stage in the process of anger control involves several options as shown on the chart. The "time out" block shown gives the client time to cool off and reduce his anger level before deciding what action, if any, to take.

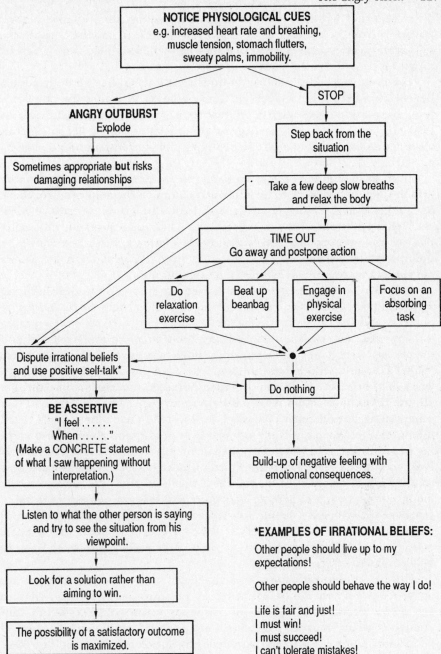

Figure 7. Anger control flow chart.

The client may literally walk away from the situation and distance himself physically from it. In order to do this, he may need to negotiate with some significant person in his life, so that that person allows him space when he asks for it.

Time out can be used either to do some thinking, to dispute irrational beliefs and use positive self-talk, or it may be used to reduce the emotional level by relaxing, by cathartic release (e.g. beating up a beanbag), by engaging in physical exercise (e.g. by going jogging) or by becoming fully absorbed in carrying out a task (e.g. putting full concentration into cooking a meal).

From this point, the options are either to do nothing further, or to move into the action described in the left-hand column on the anger control chart. Sometimes doing nothing is satisfactory. It may be that as a result of "time out" followed by one of the anger dissipating activities, the client will realize that he was over-reacting and will feel OK. However, there is a danger in doing nothing at this stage as emotions may still be bottled up with a consequent increased likelihood of a future outburst.

If "action" is the preferred option, then the first step involves disputing irrational beliefs and using positive self talk. We all at times, when angry, give ourselves messages that are destructive because they make us feel even more unhappy and angry. Such messages have been discussed in Chapter 13 and include statements like "Other people should live up to my expectations", "Other people should behave the way I do", "Life is fair and just", "I must win", "I must succeed", "I can't tolerate mistakes". Statements like this are absurd. Why should other people live up to my expectations? Who said that other people should behave the way I do? I wouldn't like other people to tell me how to behave and it is not rational for me to expect them to live up to my expectations. Life is patently not fair or just. Some people have lots of luck, and other people just don't. It isn't necessary or likely that I will always win. If I win 50 per cent of the time that would be pretty fair, and even that might not happen. So I need to remember that it is not necessary for me to win, it is not necessary for me to succeed every time, and I can, if I wish, choose to tolerate other people's mistakes. I can, if I choose, allow other people to behave in ways that are different from the ways in which I would behave myself.

Once I have put aside my irrational beliefs, I can replace them by positive ideas which will help me to feel better. For example, when someone fails to live up to my expectations I could easily say to myself, "He doesn't care enough about me to try to please me. I just don't matter to him". That would be irrational. It is just as likely that the person concerned is just a bit careless. A more positive self-statement would be "Maybe that person is naturally careless. His behaviour may have nothing to do with the way he feels about

Table 2 Comparison of anger producing irrational self-statements with positive self-statements

Irrational anger producing statement	*Equivalent positive self-statement*
1. If I don't get him to give me what I want, I'll be humiliated and made to look like a loser.	It's not reasonable to expect that I can make anyone give me what I want. I can feel proud of my ability to ask for what I want and to accept that I may not get it.
2. People should not let me down. When they let me down, I know that they don't respect me enough to want to please me.	I am a worthwhile person. It's not realistic to expect other people to live up to my expectations. When they let me down, it says more about them than me.
3. I can't feel OK unless Bill agrees that I'm right.	I can't control the way Bill thinks. If he's illogical, that's his problem, and I'm not going to make it mine. I'm OK.
4. Mary's behaviour is ruining my life. Unless she starts to do things to please me, I'm going to get very angry.	If my happiness depends on other people's behaviour, I might never be happy. I can be happy if I accept other people, including Mary, the way they are and the way they behave.
5. I've been victimized and that just isn't fair. I've got to get even.	Life often isn't fair and it's stupid to expect that it always will be. I can get on with enjoying life, instead of harbouring disturbing thoughts of revenge.

(**Note:** for other examples of irrational beliefs see Chapter 13.)

me. For all I know he might think I'm a great guy. What's more, it's not important what he thinks about me, because I know that I'm OK".

Table 2 gives some specific examples of irrational self-statements which are likely to make a person feel angry, together with alternative beliefs and positive self-statements.

Once I have translated the negative, irrational messages that I am giving myself into positive messages, then I am in a situation where I can make other positive choices. I can do nothing, at least for the time being. That is a valid choice and it may be a sensible one. Sometimes it is better to let things cool off before taking action. However, it is important to be sure not to allow negative feelings to build up as a result of inaction. If negative feelings start to build up, then they need to be dealt with and that probably means confronting the person with whom I am annoyed. Where confrontation is the choice, it needs to be done in a way which is likely to lead to a positive outcome with a minimal risk of damage to the relationship.

Constructive confrontation requires assertive rather than aggressive behaviour. An assertive person has the goal of wanting to be heard, but not the goal of definitely getting all he wants. An aggressive person is determined to win at any cost and also is intent on hurting the other person. Assertion involves communicating as an equal. It involves respecting the rights of the other person, and demands that the other person's point of view must be respected. Consequently, two assertive people may well come to the conclusion that they have different opinions. They will, however, respect the right of each other to have a different opinion. It is sufficient for the assertive person to be heard rather than to win an argument by convincing the other person to change his mind. Sometimes I will not be heard and it is not rational of me to expect that the other person will necessarily be capable of hearing me. I can accept being misunderstood if I choose to do so.

One of the best ways to make assertive statements is to use "I feel . . . when . . . " statements as explained in Chapter 18. For example, "I feel angry when you continue to smoke whilst I'm eating". By using the "I feel" statement, the speaker is owning his feelings rather than blaming the other person, and consequently he is more likely to be heard. After the feeling statement follows a concrete statement about the behaviour which caused the feeling. As explained before, it needs to be an objective statement of behaviour, and not an interpretation of the facts. By contrast with an assertive statement, an aggressive statement would be one which began with the word "you", and implied blame. For example, I could say "You are very rude because you deliberately try to annoy me by smoking when I eat". Such a statement implies blame, makes an unjustified interpretation, and is likely to lead to an argument.

The goal of making assertive statements is, of course, to get a positive outcome. After making an assertive statement, the speaker needs to listen carefully to what the other person says in reply with the intention of hearing and understanding his point of view, rather than with the intention of disputing what he says.

A good way of helping a client to practise anger control is by role-playing in front of a video camera. By video recording and role-playing a real situation which recently made the client angry, the client is able to see how other people perceive him. The client can gain if he role-plays both himself and the other person. He will need to continually change position and role to do this. A review of the video recording enables the client to see how tempers become inflamed. The counsellor can then coach the client in the anger control methods described, and in particular can teach him how to make assertive rather than aggressive statements.

Remember that very angry clients may be dangerous. As a new counsellor you need to be conscious of the need to consult with your supervisor and refer clients to other more experienced and qualified therapists when necessary. Do not attempt to do what you are not properly trained to do yourself.

Further reading on anger control

Bernstein, D. A. and Borkovec, T. D. *Progressive Relaxation Training: A Manual for the Helping Professions.* Illinois: Research Press, 1973.

Feindler, E. L. *Adolescent Anger Control: Cognitive Behavioral Techniques.* New York: Pergamon, 1986.

Hendricks, G. *Learning to Love Yourself—A Guide to Becoming Centered.* Englewood Cliffs: Prentice Hall, 1982.

Knutson, J. F. *The Control of Aggression.* Chicago: Aldine, 1973.

Novaco, R. W. *Anger Control.* Toronto: Lexington, 1975.

21   Loss and grief counselling

A high proportion of client problems are concerned with relationships. Relationship problems fall into three major categories. These are:

1. dysfunctional relationships;
2. failure to form meaningful relationships;
3. lost relationships.

The third category may either be through death or separation. Frequently marriages break up and both partners need to adjust to the loss of a spouse, the loss of marital status and the loss of the expectation that marriage is for life. If children are involved, then each parent has a loss of support from his or her spouse in the day-to-day rearing of the children, and usually one parent has a significant loss of contact with the children and suffers a feeling that the parental role is greatly diminished.

Counsellors also hear about many other types of loss, for example the loss of a limb, loss of an internal part of the body, loss of mental functioning due to ageing or brain damage, loss of a job, loss of a home, or loss of self-respect.

In order to be able to maximally help people who are grieving over a loss, counsellors need to understand the process of grieving. There are a number of books on the subject of grief counselling, and some of these are listed at the end of this chapter.

When counselling somebody who has suffered a loss, or who is grieving, it is important to be able to reassure him that the feelings that he is experiencing are normal for a person who is grieving, and that it is normal to take time to grieve. One of the most important counselling interventions for me, as a client, occurred when a counsellor self-disclosed to me that it had taken him over two years to grieve over a lost relationship. By telling me that, he helped me to feel OK, instead of believing that I was going crazy because I could not push the thoughts about a similar loss out of my mind. This example demonstrates the usefulness of appropriate counsellor self-disclosure.

Although at times self-disclosure is appropriate, it should be used sparingly, and never solely to satisfy the counsellor's needs. Before self-disclosing, examine what is going on within yourself and make a decision about whether your motive is to satisfy your own needs or is genuinely to help the client. Where self-disclosure is used more than occasionally, its impact is lost, and the counsellor is certainly putting his needs before those of the client.

When a client is grieving, use the micro-skills which you have learnt to allow the client to verbalize his thoughts and feelings, to experience rather than suppress his pain, and to generally explore whatever is happening within himself as he experiences his loss.

People tend to go through a number of stages in the grieving process. For some people these stages follow a particular sequence, but for other people the stages overlap or occur in a different order. Everyone is unique and grieves in a uniquely personal way, so do not try to fit a predetermined grieving pattern on to your client. However, if you know what the commonly experienced stages in the grieving process are, then you will be better equipped to deal with the grieving person. You will be able to explain to your client that his experiences are not strange, or unusual, but are normal for someone who is grieving.

The most important stages of grief in the usual sequence are:

- shock;
- denial;
- emotional, psychological and physical symptoms;
- depression;
- guilt;
- anger;
- idealization;
- realism;
- acceptance;
- re-adjustment;
- personal growth.

If a person is unable to work through the stages of grief, then he is likely to be stuck in a trough of hopelessness and despair. He may become neurotically obsessed by his loss, and become deeply depressed and possibly suicidal. The following paragraphs explain the stages of grief in more detail.

Usually, the first stage of grief is shock. This may be particularly severe in cases of sudden loss, or where a person has not prepared himself adequately for an expected loss. The person almost seems to stop functioning, is numb, in a daze, and is incapable of doing anything constructive. Along with shock, and following on from shock, comes denial. The grieving person can't believe that what is happening to him is really true. The denial process can be prolonged for people who separate from a living partner. Very often a rejected partner will deny that the relationship is over, even though the other partner is clearly saying, "It's finished and I'm not ever going to come back to you". This is hard to deal with because the grieving person needs to have time to move through the denial stage. Perhaps the most useful approach is to reflect back the client's expectation that his partner may return, and to add to this concrete statements of fact that seem to indicate the opposite. The counsellor might say, for example, "I get the strong impression from you that you believe that your partner will come back to you. I also notice that she said to you that she would not do that, and that she has rejected all your approaches to her since she left. Do you think that it's possible that she may not come back?". This tentative statement and question enables the client to stay in denial if he needs to do that for a while longer, or to move forward. When the client is starting to accept the possibility that the loss may be permanent, it may then be useful to let him know that denial is a normal part of grieving. By doing this he can feel OK about his difficulty in not wanting to accept reality in its entirety.

People who are dying often grieve in anticipation of dying and such people sometimes have real problems with denial. When such a person is told that he is dying he may try to convince himself that what his medical practitioner is telling him is not true. He may look for, and try, unorthodox methods to find a cure, and may start to bargain with God in an effort to get an extension on his life.

Grieving people experience feelings of depression, despair, hopelessness and worthlessness. Very often they will exhibit symptoms such as insomnia, inability to concentrate, loss of appetite and physical ill-health. This is normal. There is little that the client can do but accept that such symptoms will pass with time as the painfulness of grief diminishes.

Guilt often occurs in the grieving person. A counsellor will frequently hear a client say how guilty he feels because he didn't tell the deceased how much he loved her, didn't tell her how much he cared for her, didn't apologize for something he had done wrong, or didn't make peace over an issue where there had been a disagreement. If your clients describe such feelings, allow them to fully explore them.

Often after shock, denial, depression and guilt, anger follows. Remember though, that the stages often overlap, and sometimes a person will move forward from one stage and then go back to an earlier stage.

In the case of a person who is dying, anger may be directed at the medical practitioners. The client may feel that he hasn't had satisfactory medical treatment. Maybe he will believe that his illness was diagnosed too late and consequently that it's the doctor's fault that death is inevitable. Similarly, a person who has lost a loved one through illness may blame the medical practitioners who treated the deceased before his death. Additionally, a bereaved person may well experience anger towards the person who has died. He may feel that the deceased person "had no right to die" and has hurt him by leaving him alone to cope in the world. Often it is hard for a client to accept that he is capable of being angry towards somebody he loved and who has died. This is especially so for children who have lost a parent through death, and not had adequate counselling. They invariably feel guilty and confused by their anger and resentment towards the deceased parent. Without counselling, these feelings may endure for years.

People whose partners have rejected them often become very angry and whilst being angry, desperately want to get back into the relationship. They inevitably make it hard for themselves to do this and probably spoil their chances of reconciliation because whilst saying, "I love you and I want to be back in a relationship with you", they may also be experiencing anger, and are likely to express it in some way. Thus they give mixed messages to their partner because they are simultaneously giving "please come back" messages and angry messages. The anger, of course, can easily be understood as part of the process of grieving.

Sometimes a person who is grieving will feel angry with God, and will blame God for the loss that has occurred. For deeply religious people this may cause feelings of extreme guilt. When counselling such people explain that it is normal to experience anger in grief, and that God is quite capable of accepting, forgiving and loving someone who is angry with Him.

Idealization often follows the angry stage of grieving. It is very common for people who have suffered loss through death or separation to idealize the lost partner. The grieving person temporarily forgets any faults or negative characteristics of the deceased and remembers only an ideal person. He remembers everything positive that the deceased did and convinces himself that he loved her totally, and didn't have any negative feelings towards her. This is idealization, and once again it is normal. It takes time for a person to move through idealization and the counsellor needs to be careful not to try to move the client forward too quickly, but rather to let the grieving process occur naturally. When it is appropriate, ask tentatively whether the lost person had any bad points, any faults, or whether she sometimes made mistakes. Slowly the realization will dawn that yes, there were opposite polarities in the deceased person. She was a real person, a human being with both strengths and weaknesses.

The client will hopefully, in time, come to terms with his grief and start to accept the reality of his loss. He will start to be more realistic about the person that he has lost, and to accept his loss as a permanent reality. He is then free to move forwards and to create a new life for himself as an individual. This may be rather scary for some clients, particularly for those who were heavily dependent on the lost relationship. Now the client needs to be active rather than passive, and to try new experiences. New experiences, by their very nature, involve some degree of risk, and so may understandably cause the client to be apprehensive. Taking risks can be frightening and can also be exciting. Reframing "risk taking" as "exciting" may be helpful.

Finally, do not try to calm or soothe the grieving person. Do not try to cheer him up or help him to contain his fears. Instead, help him to express his emotions freely, to cry if he wishes, and to grieve fully. It is only when grief endures for an excessively long period, that it becomes maladaptive. In such cases, clearly professional help from an experienced counsellor, psychologist or psychiatrist is required. Once again, know the limits of your own competence, and refer clients on to others more qualified and experienced than yourself when appropriate.

Further reading on loss and grief

Kubler-Ross, E. *Death: the Final Stage of Growth.* Englewood Cliffs: Prentice Hall, 1975.

Levine, S. *Meetings at the Edge—Dialogues with the Grieving and the Dying.* New York: Anchor, 1984.

Levine, S. *Who Dies? An Investigation of Conscious Living and Conscious Dying.* New York: Anchor, 1982.

Parkes, C. M. Bereavement: Studies of Grief in Adult Life. Harmondsworth: Penguin, 1986.

Worden, J. W. *Grief Counselling and Grief Therapy.* London: Tavistock, 1986.

22 The suicidal client

My initial training as a counsellor was with a crisis telephone counselling agency. As a new telephone counsellor, my greatest fear was that I might get a call from a suicidal person. Frequently, hotline counselling services get calls from people who are contemplating suicide and sometimes such callers have already overdosed on prescribed pills before ringing for help. There are ethical issues involved when dealing with suicidal people, and before choosing strategies that are acceptable for you, you will need to clarify your own values with regard to suicide. As a counsellor, it is desirable that, if possible, you do not impose your own values on the client, that you be congruent and genuine, and that you do whatever is necessary to satisfy your own conscience. In addition, you need to be aware of any legal obligations and the legal implications of your actions. If there are internal conflicts for you when dealing with suicidal clients, then you need to resolve these for both your own and the client's well-being.

Does a person have the right to take her own life if she chooses to do so? Your answer to this question may differ from mine, and our answers may differ from the client's. I suggest that you discuss this question in depth with your training group if you are in one, or with your supervisor, so that you have a clear idea of your own attitudes and beliefs regarding suicide and of your supervisor's expectations. You will then be better equipped to deal with the suicidal client.

Some counsellors believe that a person has the right to kill herself if, after careful consideration she chooses to do so. Others strongly oppose this view and believe that firm intervention is justifiable and necessary to prevent suicide from occurring. Many counsellors believe that a person who is contemplating suicide may be temporarily emotionally disturbed and not capable of making a rational decision at that time. This belief is reinforced by experiences with clients who were suicidal and then later have thanked the counsellor, because they have found new meaning and satisfaction in their lives. Consequently, some counsellors see the need for firm intervention, involuntary hospitalization, and subsequent psychiatric treatment where other options fail. Whatever your view, suicide involves a one-way journey and suicidal clients need to be taken seriously. Remember that people who repeatedly make suicide attempts often succeed in killing themselves eventually. Their cry for help needs to be heard before it is too late.

Suicidal people broadly fall into three categories although these overlap to some extent. The first category comprises people whose quality of life is terrible, with little or no possibility for improvement. Included in this category are people who are chronically ill, in chronic pain, are seriously disabled, or are in extreme poverty with little possibility of changing their situations. Such people are often severely depressed and are seriously at risk of killing themselves because they have little to live for. This is particularly so if they are alone and do not have adequate social support systems. The second category includes people who have recently experienced a sudden trauma. These people are very much at risk during their crisis period. Included in this category are people who have suffered losses such as those described in Chapter 21. The third category comprises people who use suicidal talk or suicidal behaviour as a last resort in an attempt to get others to hear or respond to their pain. Often their goal is to manipulate the behaviour of others. They are still genuinely at risk, but their motivation is different. They often have considerable ambivalence towards dying and may not really want to die. Some people in this category are openly manipulative and, for example, might say to a spouse who has left them, "Come back to me or I will kill myself".

Here is a summary of possible reasons why a person might contemplate or talk about the possibility of killing herself:

1. Because she despairs of her situation and is unable to see an alternative solution to her problems.
2. Because she is emotionally disturbed, is afraid that she may kill herself, and wants to be stopped.
3. To make a statement.
4. As a way of hurting others; an ultimate expression of anger.
5. To make a last-ditch effort to draw attention to her seemingly impossible situation, when other methods have failed.
6. To manipulate someone else by threatening suicide.
7. Because she has positively decided to kill herself, wants to do it, and wants other people to understand the reasons for her proposed action.
8. To be in contact with another human being, prior to, or whilst, dying.
9. To say "Goodbye", as preparation for death.

Perhaps the biggest problem for a new counsellor in dealing with suicidal clients is the counsellor's own anxiety. Sometimes new counsellors try to deflect clients away from suicidal talk rather than encouraging them to bring their self-destructive thoughts out into the open and deal with them appropriately. Unfortunately, such avoidance of the issue may increase the likelihood of a suicide attempt occurring.

Whenever you are counselling a depressed or anxious client, look for the smallest clues which might suggest that the client is contemplating suicide. Clients are often reluctant to say, "I would like to kill myself". They tend, instead, to be less specific and to make statements such as "I don't enjoy life any more", or "I'm fed up with living". In such cases, be direct, and ask your client "Are you thinking of killing yourself?". In this way, suicidal thoughts are brought out into the open and can be dealt with appropriately. Remember that most people are at some times in their lives ambivalent about wanting to live and that many consider the possibility of committing suicide before rejecting it.

You will be a very unusual person indeed if your hair doesn't stand on end the first time that a client tells you that she intends to kill herself. Allow yourself to experience your feelings and then you will be able to decide what to do about them. One thing that you can do is to give yourself new messages, after discarding the irrational messages that may be contributing to your tension. Table 3 presents some typical irrational, and alternative rational self-statements for the situation.

Challenge your irrational self-statements, and if your feelings of tension don't subside then share them with the client. For example, you might say "I feel really uptight because I know that you are thinking of killing yourself. I guess it must be really scary for you too". By bringing these feelings into the open, trust can be created. A genuine and open sharing is now possible, and it is likely that the counsellor's tension will diminish.

The micro-skills which have previously been learnt, together with an appropriate counselling relationship, are the basic tools for dealing with a suicidal client. Concentrate on building the relationship and when trust has been established address the question of responsibility. The way you do this will depend on you yourself and your own value system. For myself, after I have established a good working relationship with the client I will talk with her about the responsibility of her life being, in the last resort, her own. I will explain caringly how sad it is for me to know that she is thinking about killing herself and will point out that in the long term, even though I might like to stop her, if she is seriously determined to kill herself then I will be unable to prevent her from doing so, because I can't be beside her for 24 hours each day. I will continue by telling her that I care about her even though I do not know her well, and that it is important for me to understand fully how and why she feels the way she does. I believe that by taking this approach my client will understand that she herself is responsible for her life and is likely to feel as though I am joining with her rather than pulling against her.

Table 3 Comparison between irrational and rational self-statements for counsellors dealing with suicidal clients

Irrational statement	*Rational self-statement*
I am personally responsible if this client kills herself.	Sadly, no-one can stop this client from killing herself if she firmly decides to do that. Ultimately it will be her choice.
I should stay with the client until she no longer has suicidal thoughts.	It's impossible for me to watch over the client 24 hours a day. She has to be responsible for herself. However, if I wish, and am able, I can take steps to arrange appropriate psychiatric supervision.
I have the power to change this person's mind if I am skilful enough. OR I must persuade this client not to kill herself.	I don't have the power to change someone else's mind. The most I can do is to help her explore the issues involved, and then take any other action which is available to me.
I'm not as well qualified as other counsellors.	I am me, with my skills and limitations. If I am able to refer this client on to someone more qualified I will, and in the meantime I'll do my best.
If I am incompetent I will be to blame for this person's death.	It's unrealistic for me to expect to be a perfect counsellor in such a stressful situation. I cannot take responsibility for her decision. I can only do what I am capable of doing.
I must live up to the client's expectations.	I do not need to live up to the client's expectations.
I can't cope.	I can cope provide that I set realistic expectations for myself.

For me, the biggest learning in counselling suicidal clients was to discover that if I stopped continually giving myself the message that I was responsible for the client's decision, and instead focused on the client's dilemma—"Should I kill myself or not?"—then there was the maximum possible chance of change occurring in the client's thinking. Most, if not all suicidal clients have some degree of ambivalence towards dying. After all, if a client was one hundred per cent convinced that she wanted to kill herself, she probably wouldn't be talking to a counsellor, she would just kill herself. Exploring the client's ambivalence is the key to successful counselling of such people.

As explained in Chapter 14, when a person chooses between two alternatives she loses one of the options and may also have to pay a price for the chosen option. By choosing suicide, a person loses life, contact with others and the opportunity to communicate with others about her pain. In addition she loses hope, if she had any, for a better future. The cost of dying is likely to include fear of the unknown, and for some religious people fear of being punished for killing themselves.

By joining with the client, the client is free to explore the "I want to die" part of herself with me walking alongside her in her exploration rather than pulling her away from fully exploring her negative thoughts. We will later move on together to look at the opposite part of her which still wants to continue living, or at least does not want to die.

Make your client aware of her ambivalence. Help her to look at the consequences, costs and payoffs of dying and of living. Try, if you can, to avoid directly pressuring the client to stay alive and instead help her to explore the options as fully as possible. In this way she may be able to work through her pain, and feel sufficiently valued to reconsider her decision.

An alternative approach is to try to openly persuade the client that living is the best option. This approach is not my personal preference because it sets up a struggle between the client who is saying "I want to die" and the counsellor who is saying "I want you to live". There is then heavy pressure on the counsellor to convince the client of the rightness of living, and this may be difficult as the counsellor and client are in opposition rather than joining together. Even so, this approach can be successful with some clients. There is no universal "right way" to go. Every client is unique and so is every counsellor. Choose an approach that seems right for you and your client. If you concentrate on establishing and maintaining a good relationship then you are optimizing your chances of success.

Suicidal clients are in deep depression, and depression, as explained in Chapter 18, is often due to repressed anger. Very often suicidal clients are turning anger, which could be appropriately directed at others, inward and towards themselves. It can be useful to ask the question "Who are you angry with?". If the client replies by saying "myself", you can agree that that is obvious and consistent with wanting to suicide. You might say, "You are so angry with yourself that you want to punish yourself by killing yourself". This reframe of suicide as self-punishment rather than escape may be useful in some cases in helping to produce change. You can also ask, "After yourself, who are you most angry with?". Then, if you can help the client to verbalize her anger and direct it away from herself and on to some other person or persons, her depression and suicidal thoughts may moderate.

Another way of entering the client's world is to find out what triggered off the suicidal thoughts *today*. Very often a single event is the trigger and this trigger can sometimes give important clues about the client's intentions. For example, is the client's intention partly to punish someone who has angered or hurt her? If so, there may be better ways of achieving this.

Don't forget that it is unrealistic, unfortunately, to expect that the client will necessarily decide to stay alive. Although you may be able, if you choose, to take short-term measures to ensure that she stays alive, ultimately and in the long term, if she is determined to kill herself, she is likely to succeed. However as counselling progresses you will need to decide, in consultation with your supervisor, whether direct action to prevent suicide is warranted and necessary. This decision is a heavy one and is certain to be influenced by your own values and those of the agency which employs you. There are however some cases where the decision to intervene is clear. It would, for example, be very irresponsible to allow someone who was psychologically disturbed due to a temporary psychiatric condition, or due to a sudden trauma, to kill herself without determined and positive action being taken to stop her.

A suicidal client is likely to need ongoing psychotherapy from a skilled professional, so be prepared to refer appropriately. The eventual well-being of such a client depends on her being able to make significant changes to her thinking and way of living, and this is unlikely to be achieved in one counselling session.

Further reading on suicide

Berent, I. *The Algebra of Suicide.* New York: Human Sciences, 1981.

Dunne, E. J., McIntosh, J. L. and Dunne-Maxim, K. (eds). *Suicide and its Aftermath: Understanding and Counseling the Survivors.* New York: Norton, 1987.

Fabian, S. *The Last Taboo: Suicide and Attempted Suicide Among Children and Adolescents.* Ringwood: Penguin, 1986.

Hawton K. and Catalan, J. *Attempted Suicide: A Practical Guide to its Nature and Management.* Oxford: Oxford University Press, 1987.

Lester, G. and Lester, D. *Suicide: The Gamble With Death.* Englewood Cliffs: Prentice Hall, 1971.

Stengel, E. *Suicide and Attempted Suicide.* Harmondsworth: Penguin, 1983.

PART V
Counselling practicalities

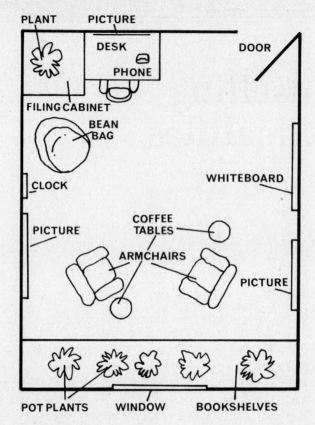

Figure 8. Counselling room arrangement.

23 Arrangement of the counselling room

Whenever I walk into a room, that room has an effect on me. Is it the same for you? Have you noticed that sometimes when you have entered a room you have felt comfortable and at ease, almost as though the room welcomed you? At other times you may have entered a room which felt clinical, cold and unwelcoming. A well designed counselling room will have a warm, friendly feel about it, to help the client feel at ease. In addition to being warm, pleasant, welcoming and comfortable, the room must be set up so that it is suitable for serious professional work.

Where a counsellor has her own personal room, that room can reflect something of her individual personality. My own room is decorated with plants and pictures. Some plants hang from macrame hangers from the ceiling, and others are arranged below a window. Pictures on the walls are peaceful, showing natural scenes of trees and landscapes. The colours are muted and not harsh, and these combine with comfortable furnishings to provide a welcoming, relaxed atmosphere.

Your room will be different from mine because you are different from me and have different tastes. Make your room an extension of yourself, so that you feel at ease in it, and then in all probability your clients will feel comfortable in it too.

Your furnishings will not be the same as mine, but ideally they should include comfortable chairs for yourself and your client, together with other furnishings appropriate for a professional office. You may need to write reports, draft letters, keep records and carry out some administrative duties. Hence a desk, telephone and filing cabinet will be required, together with bookshelves for a professional library.

The sketch in Figure 8 shows the layout of my own room. This is the room I use for my personal counselling. I also have the use of a much larger and different room, which contains video equipment, for working with couples or families. Notice that my desk and filing cabinet are unobtrusively in a corner facing the wall, where their importance for clients is diminished. I do not usually sit at the desk when clients are in the room with me. Instead I sit in an armchair, facing the client and at her own level. There is no furniture separating us. In this set-up the client may join with me as an equal partner in exploring her issues, and I hopefully am not perceived as a

145

powerful "expert" separated from my client by a desk. Even if I do need to sit at the desk to do some written work in a client's presence, the desk doesn't come between her and myself. I don't have a client chair and a counsellor chair, but rather two chairs which are similar. When a client enters the room she may sit where she chooses, but if she hesitates, I will direct her to a chair. This is a small point, but an important one. Remember that clients are usually anxious and when they enter your room, which is your space, they may be more at ease if you make it clear what is expected of them, rather than leaving them to decide what is appropriate.

My chairs are arranged so that neither chair faces directly into the light coming from the window. Looking towards a window is unpleasant, as after a while the glare will cause eye strain. During a counselling session, the client and counsellor will be looking at each other most of the time, so the background against which each is framed is really important for comfort. Preferably the client's and counsellor's chairs will face each other, but at a slight angle with enough space between them so that the client does not feel that her personal space is being invaded.

It is highly desirable to have a whiteboard in every counselling room. Clients who predominantly operate in the visual mode are likely to focus more clearly and gain in awareness if important statements are written on the board, and if their options are listed there. Sometimes a client's dilemma can be expressed through a sketch which metaphorically describes her situation. A whiteboard is particularly useful for helping clients to challenge irrational beliefs or to construct assertive statements. It may also be used as an aid when carrying out educational and administrative tasks which counsellors inevitably undertake as part of their duties.

Always have a box of tissues in a handy place in your counselling room. It is inevitable that some clients will cry and ready availability of tissues saves unnecessary embarrassment.

As will be discussed in Chapter 25, confidentiality is essential when counselling. A client will not feel comfortable about disclosing intimate personal details unless she is confident that she will not be overheard. If a client can hear voices from outside the counselling room, then she may be justified in fearing that her voice can be heard by others. Counselling rooms should therefore be suitably soundproofed.

Preferably the counselling process should be uninterrupted by the intrusion of people knocking on the door, entering the room, or phoning in unnecessarily. For this reason, many counsellors have a rule that when a counselling room door is closed, no attempt is made by others to enter the room except in extremely unusual circumstances. I have been associated for some time with an agency where, when a counselling room door is shut, the procedure for contacting the counsellor when exceptional circumstances

make this necessary, is for the receptionist to use the phone. The receptionist allows the phone to ring a few times only and if it is not answered then the counsellor is left undisturbed. This minimizes the possibility that the client might be interrupted at an important stage in the counselling process. It enables the client to feel that confidentiality is assured, and allows her to let out her emotions in privacy without the risk of being observed by others.

Setting up a counselling room gives the counsellor an opportunity to be creative, and to use her own personal ideas to generate a suitable environment in which clients may feel comfortable and do useful work. You may wish to experiment with the layout and decoration of your own room so that it becomes individually yours and welcoming to others.

24   Keeping records of counselling sessions

Many counsellors find the administrative and clerical duties associated with counselling a chore. However, it pays to keep detailed and up-to-date records on each counselling session. Ideally, report-writing should be done immediately after the counselling session, while all the relevant information is fresh in the counsellor's mind, and before other inputs have had time to intrude.

Figure 9 shows an example of a typical counsellor's record card. Notice that the client's surname appears in the top left hand corner of the card to make alphabetical filing of cards easy. The top part of the card gives factual data about the client including the client's full name, address, telephone numbers, age, marital status, name of spouse or partner, names and ages of children and referral source. Apart from essential details such as name, address and phone numbers, this part of the card is only completed if the client spontaneously divulges the necessary information during the counselling process.

The lower part of the front of the card and the back of the card are ruled so that the counsellor can write notes with regard to each interview. The notes for each counselling session may include:

1. date of the session;
2. factual information given by the client;
3. details of the client's problems, issues or dilemmas;
4. notes on the process which occurred during the session;
5. notes on the outcome of the counselling session;
6. notes on interventions used by the counsellor;
7. notes on any goals identified;
8. notes on any contract between client and counsellor;
9. notes on matters to be considered at subsequent sessions;
10. notes on the counsellor's own feelings relating to the client and the counselling process;
11. the counsellor's initials or signature.

The content of the notes will now be described in more detail under the headings listed above. However, although these headings are discussed

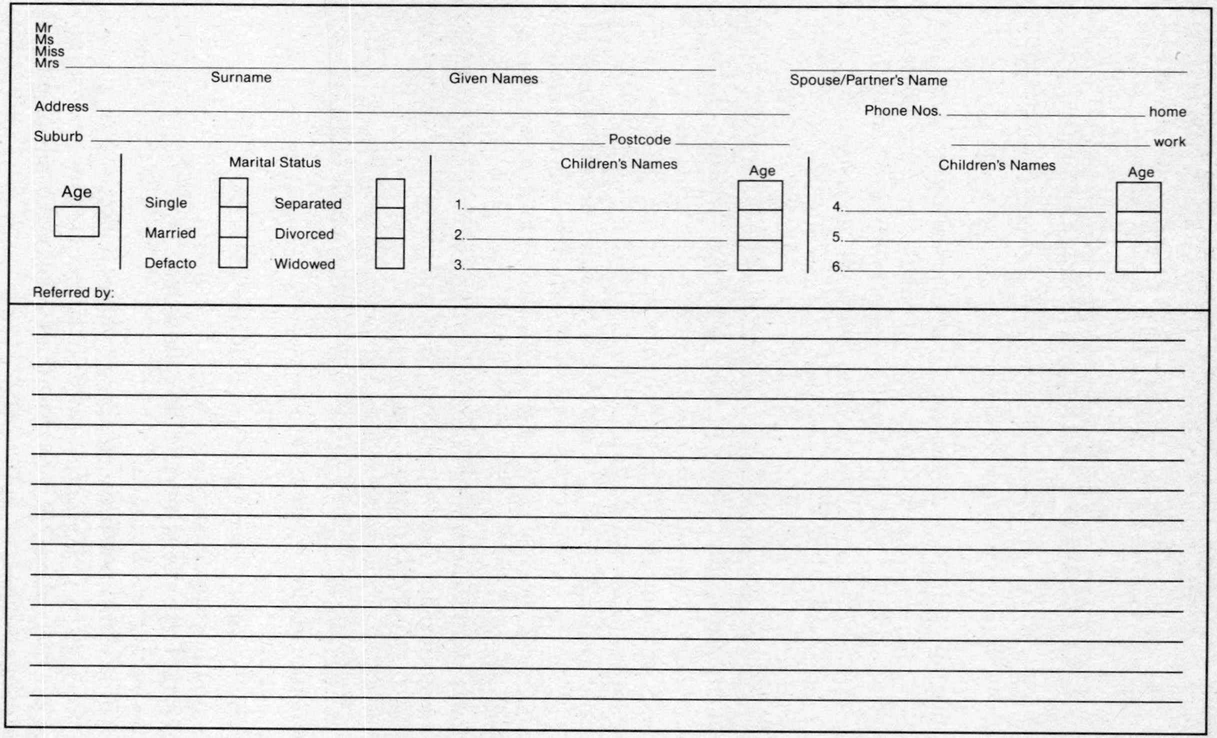
Mr
Ms
Miss
Mrs ____________________ Surname ____________________ Given Names ____________________ Spouse/Partner's Name

Address ____________________ Phone Nos. ____________________ home

Suburb ____________________ Postcode ____________ ____________________ work

Age | Marital Status: Single, Married, Defacto, Separated, Divorced, Widowed | Children's Names, Age: 1. 2. 3. | Children's Names, Age: 4. 5. 6.

Referred by:

Figure 9. Counselling record card.

individually, in practice, the notes will flow together as the headings overlap. Use the headings as a guide to stimulate and organize your thinking when report writing.

1. Date of session

This heading is self-explanatory. When reviewing a client's progress over time, it's very useful to know the dates of counselling sessions.

2. Factual information given by the client

During a counselling session the client is likely to divulge factual information which may be useful in subsequent sessions. Sometimes small facts that may appear to be insignificant provide the key to unlock a closed door in the client's world, or could, if remembered, provide the counsellor with a clearer picture of the client's background. An example of information which might be included in a counsellor's notes could be: "The client has been married for 13 years and during that time left her husband twice, once two years ago for a period of two weeks, and secondly six months ago for a longer unspecified period. She has considerable financial resources, lacks a social support system, had an affair some years ago and has kept this a secret from her husband".

3. Details of the client's problems, issues or dilemmas

Keep the record brief, so that it can be read quickly when required. An example of this part of the record would be: "Mary suspects that her husband may be sexually involved with another woman, is afraid to ask her husband whether this is so, and is confused about her attitudes to him. She can't decide whether to pluck up courage and confront him, to leave him now, or to continue in an unsatisfactory relationship with him".

4. Notes on the process which occurred during the session

The process is independent of the facts presented and of the client's issues, and is concerned with what occurred during the counselling session, particularly in the client/counsellor interaction. For example: "The client initially had difficulty talking freely, but as the counselling relationship developed she was able to explore her confusion and to look at her options. Although she was unable to decide which option to pursue, she seemed pleased by her ability to see her situation more clearly".

5. Notes on the outcome of the counselling session

The outcome could be that a decision was made, or that the client remained stuck, or that a dilemma was identified. Alternatively the outcome might be described in terms of the client's feelings at the end of the session. Examples of notes under this heading are:

"She decided to confront her husband";
"She left feeling sad and determined";
"She said that she could now see things clearly".

6.   Notes regarding interventions used by the counsellor

Notes under this section are intended to remind the counsellor of particular interventions used. For example, the notes might say:

"Taught relaxation";
"Coached client in the use of assertive statements";
"Discussed the anger control chart".

7.   Notes regarding any goals identified

These may be goals for the client to achieve in the world outside, or for her to achieve in counselling. For example:

"The client wants to learn to be more assertive";
"She wants to use the counselling process to sort out her confusion and make a decision regarding her marriage";
"She wants to experiment by taking risks".

8.   Notes regarding any contract between client and counsellor

It is important to remember any agreements that are made with clients. These may be with regard to future counselling sessions. For example:

"The client contracted to come for counselling at fortnightly intervals for three sessions and then review progress";
"It was agreed that counselling sessions would be used to explore the client's relationships with people of the opposite sex";
"I have contracted to teach the client relaxation during the next session".

9.   Notes regarding matters to be considered at subsequent sessions

Often during the last few minutes of a counselling session a client will bring up an important matter which is causing her pain and is difficult to talk about. If this is noted on the card, then the counsellor can remind the client at the start of the next session, thus enabling the client to deal with the issue in question. Sometimes, as a counsellor, you will realize at the end of a session that aspects of the client's situation need further exploration. Make a note on the card as a reminder.

10.   Notes regarding the counsellor's own feelings relating to the client and the counselling process

These are required to help the counsellor to avoid letting her feelings inappropriately interfere with the counselling process in future sessions. Such notes can be invaluable in the counsellor's own supervision and may be useful in helping her to improve her understanding of the counselling process. An example of such notes is: "I felt angry when the client continually blamed others and failed to accept responsibility for her own actions".

As stated at the start of this chapter, writing records of counselling sessions can be a chore. However, a counsellor who does this diligently will quickly become aware of the advantages. The effectiveness of future counselling sessions is likely to be improved if the counsellor reads the record card before meeting with the client each time. By doing this the counsellor is able to "tune in" to the client right from the start of the interview and will not waste time on unnecessary repetition.

Clearly, records need to be detailed and accurate if they are to be maximally useful. However, when writing records, be aware of the confidentiality issue (see Chapter 25) and of the possibility that the legal system may use its power to demand that such records be made available to the courts. Also, bear in mind when writing cards that clients may later ask to read them. Clearly clients have the right to read their own cards if they wish to do so.

Figure 10 gives an example of a completed record card. This example is fictitious and does not relate to any living person.

Mr ~~Mrs~~ ~~Miss~~

HARDTRIER | **BRENDON** | **URSULA**
Surname | Given Names | Spouse/Partner's Name

Age: 40?

Address _____
Suburb: Mount Carina _____ Postcode _____ Phone Nos. _____ home _____ work

Marital Status

Single ☐	Separated ☐	
Married ☐	Divorced ☐	
Defacto ☑	Widowed ☐	

Children's Names

Children's Names	Age
1. ? (Ursula's child)	19
2. Janet (Ursula's child)	16
3. ? (Brendan's child)	?
4. Paul (Brendan's child)	10?
5.	
6.	

Referred by: Kathy Doolette of the Kerala Community Service

18/5/88 Brendon lives with Ursula, his two children, and his two children. He has lived in this suburb/vicinity for the past 3 years. He works as a gardener and enjoys his job.

Brendon appeared to be extremely anxious throughout the session and he described his high anxiety level as his main problem. He could see no reason for this anxiety and told me that his life was in many ways a good one. As our relationship developed he started to talk about the past and became very distressed when talking about his ex-wife. The rest of the session was spent working on his grief due to the loss of what he considered to be a good marriage.

At the end of the session Brendon told me that he felt he had just "scratched the surface" of his problems. We made a contract for him to come weekly for three more sessions if necessary and then to review the situation. RAH

27/5/88 Brendon appeared to be far more relaxed when he arrived for the session, and told me that during the past week he had talked with Ursula about his feelings of loss. She

P.T.O.

Figure 10A. Completed record card—front.

had this shared some of his issues with him and the exchange had brought them closer. He now realises that much of his anxiety relates to feelings of insecurity in his relationship with Ursula.

Gordon explored his feelings of insecurity and became aware that partly they come from past experience and partly from difficulties in relating to Ursula. At the end of the session he decided to ask Ursula to join with him in having relationship counselling instead of him continuing with an original contract. *RH.*

Figure 10B. Completed record card—rear.

25 Confidentiality and professional ethics

The first part of this chapter will be devoted exclusively to confidentiality, because it is one of the most important ethical issues for a counsellor. Other aspects of professional ethics will be considered in the second part of the chapter.

Confidentiality

For counselling to be maximally effective, the client must feel secure in the knowledge that what he tells the counsellor is to be treated with a high degree of confidentiality. Ideally, a client would be offered total confidentiality, so that he would feel free to openly explore with the counsellor the darkest recesses of his mind, and to discuss the most intimate details of his thoughts. As a new counsellor I naively believed that I could at all times give my clients an assurance that what was said in the counselling session was between them and me and would not be discussed with others. I very soon learnt that this was an idealistic belief and found that in practice it is not always possible to provide total confidentiality. As a counsellor you may at times be faced with some personal difficulties regarding confidentiality. You need to give your client an assurance that what he says will be in confidence, because unless you are able to do that the client is unlikely to be open with you. However, you also need to be aware of the limits to the confidentiality which you are offering.

There are several instances where total confidentiality is either impossible, undesirable or unethical. These include the following:

1. the need to keep records;
2. the requirements of professional supervision;
3. where others need to be protected;
4. when working in conjunction with other professionals;
5. when participating in educational training programs, conferences, workshops and seminars;
6. in cases where the law requires disclosure of information.

The above list will now be discussed in detail. As explained in Chapter 24 there are compelling reasons for keeping good records. Counsellors who work in agencies frequently use centralized filing systems for such records. This makes it possible for other counsellors and non-counselling staff such as receptionists and filing clerks to have access to confidential records. Some counsellors omit to note certain categories of sensitive material on their record cards as a way of protecting clients. However, there are obviously consequences if this policy is adopted, as important information may be overlooked or forgotten during subsequent counselling sessions. Clearly, for the protection of clients, record cards should not be left lying around in places where they can be read by unauthorized people, and all records should be stored in a lockable filing cabinet or filing room.

The requirements of professional supervision, as described in Chapter 26, demand that counsellors be free to fully disclose client material to their supervisors. This is essential if clients are to receive the best possible service, and is also necessary for the well-being of counsellors themselves. Some counsellors openly talk with their clients about the requirements of professional supervision and sometimes it can be re-assuring for a client to know that his counsellor is receiving supervision. Other counsellors maintain secrecy about their own supervision in order to give their clients a fuller sense that counselling is in confidence.

Experienced counsellors sometimes work with dangerous clients, or with clients who have committed serious offences against other people and may possibly repeat such behaviour. Clearly, counsellors have responsibilities not only to their clients, but also to the community. There may be instances where a counsellor needs to divulge information to protect a third party. For example, if a counsellor knows that his client possesses a gun and intends to kill someone, then it would be unethical and irresponsible if the person at risk, the police or the psychiatric authorities were not informed. Where there is doubt about the desirability of informing others, then the counsellor needs to consult with his supervisor.

Professionals such as psychiatrists, medical practitioners, psychologists, social workers, clergy and welfare workers, frequently phone counsellors to talk with them about mutual clients. It is sometimes important for the welfare of such clients that other professionals are appropriately informed about their situations. It is also desirable for counsellors to maintain good working relationships with other helping professionals. Sensible judgments need to be made about what information is disclosed and what is withheld. If you believe that it is desirable that sensitive material be disclosed, then obtain the client's permission first, unless there are unusual and compelling reasons for not doing so. To a new counsellor it probably seems undesirable and unnecessary to ever allow the sharing of such information. However, consider the following example. Imagine that a client comes to see you and that a psychiatrist who is treating another member of the family gives you some helpful and useful information, and asks you to help him by confirming that his perception of the family situation is accurate. It may well be advantageous, in the therapeutic management of both clients, if you work co-operatively with the psychiatrist. In such an instance, it could be appropriate to obtain client permission, and to keep the client informed of ongoing contact with the psychiatrist.

Where two members of a family require counselling help, the need for family therapy is usually indicated. However if family therapy is not available, or is considered inappropriate, then any helping professionals involved with members of the family are likely to achieve more for their clients if they consult with each other, have case conferences and work together as a team.

Sometimes you may discover that a client of yours is also consulting with another counselling professional. There is rarely justification for two counsellors working with the same client, and so after discussion with the client it is sensible to contact the other counsellor to decide who will take over the case. There are exceptions to most rules, and sometimes if good contact is maintained between two counsellors it may be possible for them both to remain involved provided that each sets clear boundaries and goals for their individual work.

Another problem area regarding confidentiality concerns ongoing training, upgrading of skills and sharing of new techniques. Counsellors need to grow and develop as people and counsellors. This can partly be done through personal supervision and partly through large group sharing at conferences, seminars, workshops and case conferences. Client material that is presented at such events can sometimes be disguised by changing names and other details, but often this is not possible, particularly when video recordings of counselling sessions are used. Client material should never be used in this way without the prior written consent of the client, as described in Chapter 26. Moreover there could be legal problems if consent is not obtained.

Remember that client confidentiality may be limited by legal intervention. Sometimes counsellors are subpoenaed to give evidence in court and in such cases withholding information may be contempt of court.

Clearly, from the preceding discussion, there are many reasons why confidentiality in the counselling situation is limited. However, it is your task to ensure that client confidentiality is preserved as far as is possible. Assure your clients that you will do this to the best of your ability, because they need to feel that whatever they share with you is protected information which will not be carelessly or unnecessarily divulged to others. It is quite unethical to talk about clients or client material to any person whatsoever, except in the

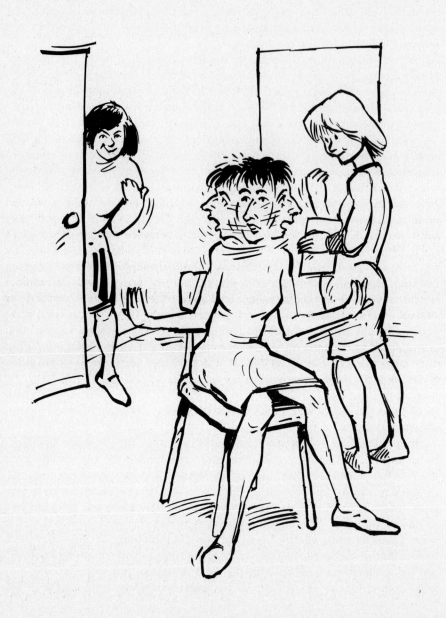

circumstances previously described in this chapter. What a client shares with you is his personal property and must not be shared around, so if you do have a need to talk about a client or his issues then talk with your supervisor.

You will need to make your own decisions about how to deal with the confidentiality issue. My own policy is to wait until a client raises the issue of confidentiality, if he does. I will then say, "What you say to me here is between you and me". If at a later stage I need to divulge information to someone else for an ethically acceptable and professional reason, then I will ask the client's permission to do this. The only exception to this rule for me is when a third party is in danger, in which case I will be direct and open with the client about my intentions. This policy ensures maximum client and community protection.

I am good at keeping secrets, are you?

Professional ethics

The issue of confidentiality has been discussed in some detail. However, there are many other ethical issues for counsellors, and a new counsellor needs to be informed of these. Many counsellors belong to professional associations which have codes of ethical conduct. These codes are readily available on request, and it is sensible for a new counsellor to read through the relevant code for her profession. Some of the more important ethical issues are included in the list below, and these will be discussed in subsequent paragraphs:

1. respect for the client;
2. responsibility of the counsellor;
3. counsellor competence;
4. referral;
5. limits of the client/counsellor relationship;
6. self-promotion;
7. termination of counselling;
8. legal obligations.

1. Respect for the client
Regardless of who the client is, and regardless of her behaviour, the client has come to you for help, and deserves to be treated as a human being of worth. If you treasure your client, then she will, through feeling valued, be given the optimum conditions in which to maximize her potential as an individual. Within each one of us is the potential for good, and for that potential to be realized we need to feel OK about ourselves. Counsellors have

a responsibility to help their clients to feel OK about themselves, and to increase their feelings of self-worth.

If you try to impose your own moral values on the client, then you are likely to make her feel judged and to damage her self-worth. Moreover, she is likely to reject you as a counsellor and to reject your values too. Paradoxically, if you are able to accept your clients, with whatever values they have, you may well find that as time passes they move closer to you in their beliefs. This is inevitable, because as counsellors we are, whether we like it or not, models for our clients. We have a responsibility to be good models.

The client's interests must take precedence over the counsellor's during the counselling process. It is not ethical to use a counselling session with a client to work through your own issues. The correct time for working through your issues is in a supervision session.

2.   Responsibility of the counsellor

Counsellors frequently experience a sense of conflict between their responsibilities to the client, to the employing agency and to the community. You will at times need to make your own decisions about which of these responsibilities needs to take precedence, and in my view the decision is unlikely to always be the same. If you are in doubt about any particular decision, consult your supervisor.

Generally, the counsellor's responsibility to the client must take precedence. The client has come to you for confidential help, and so you have an implied contract with her to give her that, unless you tell her something to the contrary. Clearly though, you cannot ethically fulfil her needs if doing so would:

1. involve working in opposition to the policies of the organization which employs you;
2. involve a breach of the law;
3. put other members of the community at risk;
4. be impossible for you personally.

However, in these situations you need to be clear with your client about your own position, so that she understands the conditions under which she is talking to you.

Counsellors who are employed by an organization or institution have a responsibility to that employing body. All the work they do within that organization or institution needs to fulfil the requirements of the employing body, and to fit in with the philosophical expectations of the employing body. For example, I am employed by Lifeline Brisbane, an organization which comes under the umbrella of the Uniting Church in Australia. It is my responsibility to carry out my work at Lifeline within the framework of the Christian tradition. If I were not able to do that, then I would have an ethical responsibility to discuss the issue with my employers.

Counsellors, at all times, have to be aware of their responsibilities to the community at large. As discussed earlier in this chapter, this raises problems with regard to confidentiality. Whenever a member of the community is at risk, property is likely to be damaged, or other illegal actions are likely to occur, or have occurred, then you have an obligation to the community to take appropriate action. However, most decisions do not involve choosing between black and white, but rather between shades of grey, and sometimes you may find it difficult to decide what is most appropriate, in order to serve the needs of the community in the long term. At these times the sensible approach is to talk through the ethical issues with your supervisor.

3. Counsellor competence

A counsellor has a responsibility to ensure that she gives the highest possible standard of service. This cannot be done without adequate training and supervision. All counsellors need to attend to their own professional development (see Chapter 26), and to have supervision from another counsellor on a regular basis. Failure to do this is certain to result in the counsellor's own issues intruding into the counselling process to the detriment of the client.

A counsellor also needs to be aware of the limits of her competence. We all have limits professionally and personally, and it is essential that as counsellors we are able to recognize our limits and to be open with our clients about those limits. The client has a right to know whether she is seeing someone who has, or does not have, the abilities necessary to give her the help she requires.

4. Referral

When a client's needs cannot be adequately met by a counsellor, then that counsellor has a responsibility to make an appropriate referral, in consultation with the client, to another suitable professional. However, it is possible for a counsellor to avoid all difficult and unenjoyable work by excessively referring clients to others. Clearly there is a responsibility on all counsellors to carry a fair load, and to be sensible about referral decisions. Such decisions are best made in consultation with a supervisor.

Rather than referring, it may sometimes be appropriate for the counsellor to continue seeing the client herself, whilst under intensive supervision. If this happens, then the counsellor has a responsibility to inform the client.

When referring clients to others, good professional conduct demands that you contact the professional to whom the referral is being made, with the client's permission, to ensure that the referral is acceptable and appropriate.

5.   Limits of the client/counsellor relationship

In all our relationships we set limits. Each of us has a boundary around ourself which preserves our identity as an individual. The strength of that boundary, and its nature, depends on who the relationship is with, and on the context of the relationship. The client/counsellor relationship is a special type of relationship which is established by the client for a particular purpose. The client enters into the relationship, entrusting the counsellor with her well-being, and expecting that the counsellor will, throughout the relationship, provide her with a safe environment in which she can work on her problems.

As discussed previously, the client/counsellor relationship is not an equal relationship, and inevitably, whether the counsellor wishes it or not, she is in a position of power and influence. She is often working with clients who are in a highly emotional state and are consequently very vulnerable. The way in which a counsellor relates to a client is uncharacteristic human behaviour. A counsellor devotes most of her energy into listening to and understanding the client, and so the client sees only a part of the counsellor's character. Inevitably, a client is likely to see a counsellor as unrealistically caring and beautiful. The counsellor's power and the client's biased perception combine to make the client very vulnerable to offers of friendship or closeness.

The counsellor is also vulnerable. In the counselling relationship, the client often shares her innermost secrets, and so inevitably there may develop a real closeness between the client and counsellor. Counsellors learn to be empathic, and so they develop special relationships with their clients. If they are not careful they too become vulnerable to offers of closer relationships than are appropriate.

Unfortunately, it is almost always unhelpful, and often damaging to the client, when the client/counsellor relationship is allowed to extend beyond the limits of the counselling situation. If such an extension occurs, the counsellor's ability to attend to the client's needs is seriously diminished, and there may well be serious psychological consequences for the client.

As a counsellor, it may at times be hard to refuse invitations to get closer to your clients than the counselling situation allows. Remember that if you do not set appropriate boundaries you will merely be satisfying your own needs at the expense of the client. You will have abused your special position of trust as a professional, and you will have to live with that knowledge, and with any more serious consequences. Be aware of the danger signals when your relationship with a client is becoming too close, and bring the issue into the open by discussing it with your supervisor and with the client, if that is appropriate.

6. Self-promotion

Most professional associations for counsellors have specific rules about advertizing. There is clearly an ethical issue with regard to the way in which counsellors describe themselves and their services. It is unethical for a counsellor to make claims about herself or her services which are inaccurate or cannot be substantiated. Counsellors who do this not only put their clients at risk, but may also face the possibility of prosecution.

7. Termination of counselling

As discussed in Chapter 16, termination of counselling needs to be carried out sensitively and with appropriate timing. It is not ethical to terminate counselling at a point where the client still needs further help. If for some unavoidable reason (e.g. such as leaving the district) you need to do this, then it is encumbent upon you to make a suitable referral to another counsellor who can continue to give the necessary support.

8. Legal obligations

Counsellors, like all other professionals and every other member of the community, need to operate within the law. As a counsellor, you therefore need to familiarize yourself with the relevant legal requirements for your profession.

PART VI
The counsellor's own needs

26 Supervision and ongoing training

Clients are people with real needs. They need to be valued and given the best available help. It is therefore not ethical for a client to be seen by a new counsellor unless that counsellor is being adequately supervised. There are a number of ways in which supervision can occur:

1. by direct observation with the supervisor in the counselling room;
2. by direct observation through a one-way mirror;
3. by observation using a closed circuit TV;
4. by use of an audio or video recording;
5. by means of a verbatim report.

These methods will be discussed in turn.

Trainee counsellors are usually apprehensive about seeing their first few clients. A good way to help them adjust to the counselling environment is for trainees to sit in on counselling sessions conducted by their supervisors. Naturally, the permission of the client is required. Student counsellors who are allowed to do this need to understand what their supervisor expects of them. Initially, I prefer my students to take a low profile and to sit quietly out of the line of vision of the client. This reduces the necessity for the client to feel the need to interact with two counsellors simultaneously, leaves me free to conduct the session in the way that I choose, and enables the trainee to observe without feeling pressured to participate. As the trainee's level of comfort increases, some participation by her can occur. Adopting this approach allows her to observe me as a model, and to feel at ease with a client and myself in the room. The method allows the trainee to gradually make the transition from being a passive observer to being an active counsellor under supervision.

The process just described is excellent for raw beginners who have had no previous counselling experience but there are problems connected with having both the trainee and supervisor in the room together. Obviously, some of the intimacy of the counselling relationship is lost, and as a consequence the client may find it difficult to deal openly with sensitive issues. Also the supervisor will inevitably be involved in the counselling process even after the trainee has substantially taken over as counsellor. This will make it difficult for the supervisor to recognize, in an objective way, what is happening in the counselling process. It is essential that she is able to do this, if she is to give accurate feedback to the trainee.

The one-way mirror system as shown in Figure 11 provides a better alternative. Many counselling centres have a pair of adjacent rooms set up like this for training purposes, and for family therapy. The one-way mirror allows a person in the observation room to watch what is happening in the counselling room without being seen. A microphone, amplifier and speaker system provide sound for the observer, so that she is able to see and hear what is happening. Ethically, it is imperative that a client who is being observed from behind a one-way mirror is informed in advance about the presence of the observer, or observers, and that consent is obtained for the session to proceed in this way.

The one-way mirror system can initially be used to enable a trainee or trainees to watch an experienced counsellor at work. Later the trainee can work as a counsellor whilst being observed by her supervisor, and possibly by other trainees also. The system has the advantage that the supervisor is not present in the counselling room and therefore does not intrude on the counselling process. However, she is available to take over from the trainee if that becomes necessary, and she can give objective feedback after the session is completed.

A similar method to the one-way mirror system is to have a video camera in the counselling room connected to a TV monitor in another room. However this method doesn't provide as much visual detail as is obtained with the one-way mirror system.

One of the best methods of supervision is by use of video recordings. Audio recordings could also be used although their usefulness is very limited because non-verbal behaviour cannot be observed. Video recordings of counselling sessions are a rich source of information. Not only may selected segments of a session be viewed repeatedly, but it is also possible to freeze the picture so that non-verbals may be studied. Whenever an audio or video recording is made it is essential to obtain the prior written consent of the client, and to tell him who will have access to the recording and when it is to be erased. Many agencies have standard consent forms for clients to sign. It is sensible to have such forms checked for their legal validity.

A combination of a one-way mirror system, video camera and video recorder is a very powerful arrangement for counsellor training. Trainees can be directly observed during practice sessions, and may later process their work with their supervisors by reviewing the video-recordings.

Another method of supervision is by use of the verbatim report. A verbatim report is a written report which records word for word, the client's statements and the counsellor's responses. It may be produced from

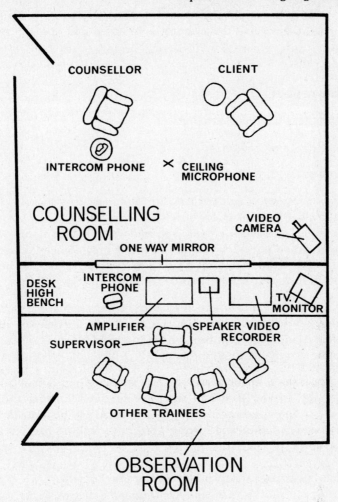

Figure 11.   Counselling and observation rooms.

memory, or as a transcript of an audio recording. Here is an example of a verbatim report. Note that this example is invented and does not relate to a real client.

Verbatim report

NAME OF COUNSELLOR: Fiona Newhelper

NAME OF CLIENT: Simon Sadperson

DATE OF COUNSELLING SESSION: 19.8.89

BACKGROUND INFORMATION ABOUT THE CLIENT: Simon is 36 years old, has been married twice and has two children. These are a girl, 12, and a boy, 10. Both children are in the custody of Simon's second wife. He lives alone.

This was Simon's second visit to see me. He came a week ago feeling tense and depressed. He told me that he was worried about his inability to build relationships with women, and he couldn't understand why.

MY FEELINGS AND ATTITUDES PRIOR TO THE SESSION: I was feeling good myself and was looking forward to working with this client again. I believed that I had built a good relationship with him during the previous session and that this would enable him to talk freely with me.

WHAT OCCURRED PRIOR TO THE RESPONSES GIVEN BELOW: When Simon arrived for this session he looked pale and was very subdued. During the first 15 minutes of our time together his body looked tense and he seemed reluctant to talk. After a few minutes of silence, I felt as though he had put a barrier between us and I spoke.

F1.   Seems like there's a barrier between us. (Said quietly.)
S1.   Ah what . . . what da ya mean? (He sounded defensive to me.)
F2.   Like we're separated by a barrier. (I used my hands to suggest a barrier.)
S2.   Separated? (Said with non-verbals that suggested disbelief and questioning. I felt very shut out from Simon now.)
F3.   Yes, I feel shut out by an invisible barrier. Sometimes you open it up a . . . (Simon interrupted heatedly.)
S3.   No, no, it's a double brick wall with a door in it. The door is usually closed and that's because it keeps me safe.
F4.   That brick wall's important to you!
S4.   It sure is!
F5.   It protects you. (Simon started to talk freely and easily after this.)

S5.　Yes, it does . . . (He went on to explain how vulnerable he would feel without the wall, and then started to cry. I waited.)

　　　. . . You see, I've been hurt too much in the past, and I'm scared that if I'm me, if I'm really me, and open up, then I'll be rejected again.

F6.　The barrier protects you from the pain of rejection. (Long pause.)

S6.　It also prevents me from getting into a relationship and I'm not sure that I like that. (Said carefully, slowly, and firmly.)

F7.　You don't sound sure about whether you want the barrier or not.

S7.　Well, it would be hard to tear it down. I'm so used to it now. You know I realize that the barrier's been there for a long time now. Goodness knows what might happen if I didn't have it there.

F8.　It would be risky to tear it down.

S8.　It would. (He paused to think for what seemed a long time. I had difficulty staying silent because I wanted to tell him what he was discovering for himself.) . . . You know, I would get hurt for sure, and what's worse, I'd have to take responsibility for the ways I hurt the women I get close to. (He laughed.) That's worse. That's worse! I can't bear it when I hurt someone I love.

F9.　Getting close involves lots of hurt. (He interrupted, fortunately, before I was able to take him off track by suggesting getting close could also involve pleasure. I was bursting to tell him!)

S9.　Yes, it seems like that to me . . . (He then told me in detail about his pain at losing his second wife. He couldn't understand how he hurt so much when he had left her.) . . . It's not over yet. How can I still be hurting after so long?

F10.　I get the impression that you're still grieving.

S10.　I should be over her by now! (Said despairingly.)

F11.　It takes time to grieve. Can you give yourself time?

From here on the process flowed naturally as he dealt with his grief. I got the strong feeling that his barrier would gradually disintegrate as he worked through his grief.

MY FEELINGS AFTER THE SESSION: I felt good because Simon had moved forwards to a fuller awareness of himself and his behaviour. I felt I had been infected by some of his sadness though.

WHAT I HAVE LEARNT FROM THE SESSION (OR THINGS I'D DO DIFFERENTLY ANOTHER TIME): I learnt that it was helpful for the client when I shared with him my own feelings (of separation, see F1, F2 and F3). Because he interrupted (F9 and S9), I discovered that it was better to follow his path. If I had brought the focus on to the pleasure associated with closeness then I would have made it more difficult for him to address the underlying issue of his grief. I learnt that my desire "to make the client feel good" could have been counter-productive. I'm pleased he interrupted and prevented me from doing this.

Fiona Newhelper

As you will see from the above example of a verbatim report, the report begins with background information about the client, his problems and his emotional state. The first part of the report may also summarize the process and outcome of previous counselling sessions.

The next section of the report concerns the counsellor's own feelings and attitudes prior to the counselling session. This information is required because a counsellor's behaviour and performance is often influenced by her mood, feelings generally and feelings towards the client, and her preconceived ideas and attitudes concerning the client and the client's behaviour.

A central component of the verbatim report is the section containing client statements and counsellor responses. This section usually contains only about 10 to 20 responses from each person. It would be very laborious to write out a transcript of a substantial part of a counselling interaction and this is unnecessary. Preferably the trainee counsellor will select a portion of the session which demonstrates some important learning, or highlights some difficulties. Often a new counsellor will find that a part of the interaction seems to "go wrong" inexplicably. Such a segment provides ideal material for a verbatim report and subsequent discussion in supervision. Notice that responses are numbered and identified by the initial letter of the person's name. For example, statement F7 is Fiona's seventh in the report. After each statement, in parentheses, is recorded other significant information, including non-verbal behaviour, silences and the feelings and thoughts of the counsellor.

Immediately before the verbatim client and counsellor statements is a description of what occurred in the session prior to them, and immediately after them is a brief description of what occurred in the remaining part of the session. These descriptions are required so that the statements that are recorded verbatim are seen in the context of the whole session.

The verbatim report concludes with sections which describe the counsellor's feelings after the session and her learnings for the future. It is then signed.

Verbatim reports enable a supervisor to tap into trainee issues which might have blocked her from satisfactorily helping the client to work through his issues. Such reports also enable the supervisor to identify inappropriate counsellor responses and to help the trainee discover better ones.

Audio-recordings, video-recordings and verbatim reports require the same level of protection as client records in order to ensure that confidentiality is preserved. It is essential that tapes and reports are not left in places where they might fall into the hands of unauthorized persons.

By using any of the methods which have been described in this chapter, a supervisor can help a new counsellor to improve her skills and to understand the process which occurred during a particular counselling session. Often, understanding this process will involve the trainee in an exploration of her own issues, because these issues are likely to have influenced the way she responded to the client. A counsellor will feel emotional pain when her client discusses issues which are similar to unresolved emotional issues of her own. Consequently, when issues are discussed that are painful for the counsellor herself, then she may well avoid her own pain, either by steering the client in another direction, or by attempting to encourage the client to pursue a course of action which in some way satisfies the counsellor's own needs. A perceptive supervisor will spot counsellor behaviour which demonstrates avoidance of painful issues and will ask the trainee to explore whatever it was that was happening emotionally within her, when the avoidance occurred.

Most people don't look closely at their own emotional problems unless they are causing them considerable distress. It is a natural human defence to suppress uncomfortable feelings and not to delve into them without good reason. However, a counsellor must delve into uncomfortable feelings, because if I as a counsellor have a problem that I can't face, then it will be quite impossible for me to help a client with a similar problem. As counsellors therefore, we need to explore and deal with all of our own painful issues as they come into our awareness. The spin-off for us is that our personal growth is enhanced when we do this.

This chapter has discussed ways in which you may be supervised as a new counsellor. Your initial training is just the beginning, and there is no end to the ongoing need for further training. A good counsellor never stops learning from her own experiences and from what others can teach her. In order to improve, it is advantageous to continue in supervision, even when an experienced counsellor.

The counselling strategies described in this book are the basic ones. Once you have mastered them, continue to study under experienced counsellors who have advanced skills or who are skilled in specialist therapeutic methods. There are many different therapies suitable for use by counsellors. These include Gestalt Therapy, Rational Emotive Therapy, Cognitive Behavioural Therapy, Neuro Linguistic Programming, Reality

Therapy and Provocative Therapy. I personally use an eclectic approach, although I put an emphasis on Rogerian methods during the early stages of a counselling relationship, and on Gestalt Therapy as the relationship grows, when working with individuals.

If you move on from working as a counsellor with individuals to doing marital or family therapy, then you will need to know about the various systems approaches such as Strategic Family Therapy, Conjoint Family Therapy and Structural Family Therapy.

Your ongoing training can best be carried out through experiential training in workshops and seminars, together with hands-on experience under the supervision of a qualified and experienced practitioner.

Suggested reading on various therapies

Bandler, R. *Using Your Brain for a CHANGE—Neuro-Linguistic Programming.* Moab: Real People Press, 1985.

Burns, D. D. *Feeling Good—The New Mood Therapy.* New York: Signet, 1980.

Corsini, R. J. *Current Psychotherapies.* Itasca: Peacock, 1979.

Ellis, A. and Harper, R. A. *A New Guide to Rational Living.* Hollywood: Wilshire Book Company, 1975.

Farelly, F. and Brandsma, J. *Provocative Therapy.* California: Meta, 1982.

Glasser, W. *Reality Therapy.* New York: Harper Colophon, 1975.

Polster, E. and Polster, M. *Gestalt Therapy Integrated.* New York: Vintage, 1974.

27 The counsellor's own well-being

A counsellor's own well-being is of paramount importance, because if he is not feeling good he is unlikely to be fully effective. For a counsellor to feel good he must resolve his own personal issues satisfactorily. This can be done as described in the previous chapter, through regular supervision from an experienced counsellor. Counselling can be draining, so counsellors need support, otherwise they are likely to find themselves emotionally depleted.

In recent years, it has become clear that all counsellors at times experience what is known as "burnout". Burnout is disabling, but if it is recognized in its initial stages, then it is comparatively easy to take remedial action. Even experienced counsellors fail at times to recognize the onset of burnout and try to convince themselves that the symptoms which they are experiencing are due to some other cause. It is difficult for many counsellors to admit to themselves, let alone to others, that they are burning out, even though there is now general acceptance that burnout is a common problem for counsellors. The first step in dealing with burnout is to be aware of the symptoms.

There is a wide range of symptoms which come under the general heading of burnout. These symptoms give an indication that the counsellor is becoming drained emotionally by his counselling work and is wanting to draw back. He may experience a feeling of being totally overworked and of having no control over his workload. He may perceive himself as swimming against the tide and unable to keep his head above water. This leads to feelings of hopelessness and helplessness.

Counsellors experiencing burnout are usually tired physically, emotionally and mentally. They start to feel that they can't face meeting with another client. Typically, a counsellor may say to himself during a counselling session, "I really can't bear to be here. I wish the client would just go away". He may experience being physically debilitated and find it hard to drag himself to work. His enthusiasm has evaporated and he may have physical symptoms such as headaches, stomach-aches, skin disorders, high blood pressure or back and neck pains. His susceptibility to viruses and other infections is increased.

The burnt-out counsellor may develop strong negative attitudes towards clients. He may develop a cynical attitude to his clients and blame them for

creating their own problems. He may even start to treat his clients in an impersonal way, as though they were objects and not human beings. Consequently, the counselling relationship will suffer and counselling becomes a chore, rather than an interesting, challenging and creative activity. The counsellor clearly no longer finds satisfaction in his work. Negative attitudes may also be experienced towards fellow workers, supervisors, other staff and towards the employing organization.

Disillusionment with the counselling process is a major burnout symptom. Counsellors start to question the value of their work and begin to wonder whether what they're doing is worthwhile. A burnt out counsellor will often be unable to see any evidence of success in his work. He feels frustrated by his inability to bring about change in his clients and is dissatisfied with his job, believing that it involves giving and getting nothing in return. This leads to feelings of failure and low self-esteem. The demands of clients become too great and the counsellor may just want to withdraw from the helping situation. In the advanced stages of burnout, the counsellor starts taking days off sick, and may start frantically looking for a new job so that he can resign.

One of the sad consequences of burnout is that it invariably affects the counsellor's personal life. As his self-esteem diminishes, his personal relationships are put in jeopardy, and other people become targets for feelings of anger, frustration, helplessness and hopelessness.

What is the primary cause of burnout? Well, it seems likely that it results from the stress of the interpersonal counselling relationship. This is an unbalanced relationship, with the counsellor doing most of the giving and the client doing most of the receiving.

In the early chapters of this book, heavy emphasis was put on establishing an empathic relationship, and on the need to join with the client. It is essential, that as a counsellor, you learn to do this effectively, because *empathy* is one of the essential ingredients of successful counselling. However, *being empathic can be hazardous to a counsellor's health!* That is, unless proper precautions are taken.

Clients are often in a highly emotional state, and if a counsellor listens with empathy and effectively joins with an emotional client, then the counsellor himself is likely to be infected by the client's emotional state. Emotions, like viruses, are catching, which is probably why people who aren't counsellors try to calm their friends down when they are emotional. After all, who wants to be emotionally distressed? In contrast to most friends, counsellors encourage people to experience and express their emotions fully. Empathic counsellors are certain to experience, at some level, emotions similar to those of their clients. Clearly, no counsellor can afford to be emotionally distressed for a significant part of his working day, because to allow this to happen would be certain to result in burnout. Counsellors who are working mainly with emotionally disturbed clients are therefore very much at risk and need to take special precautions to avoid burnout.

With experience, you will learn how to walk beside a client with empathy and also how to protect yourself from the excesses of emotional pain by at times moving back for a while, grounding yourself, and then joining more fully with the client again. Certainly, if you are to protect yourself from burnout, you will need to learn how to do this. I will describe the technique which I use for myself, and then you will need to experiment for yourself, to find out what works best for you.

In a counselling session, when I notice that I am starting to *excessively* experience a client's emotional pain, I immediately set about grounding myself. This grounding process takes only a second or two to happen, but will take longer to describe.

I imagine myself to be encapsulated by a plastic space-bubble which separates me from outside emotions, but enables me to observe them, and allows me to respond to them appropriately. I then slow down my breathing, and relax my body, so that my troubled emotional state is replaced by tranquillity. In my imagination, I float, in the space-bubble, upwards and backwards to a position about five metres behind and above my body. It is as though the part of me in the bubble is able to observe both the client and the physical me, which is still sitting in my counselling chair. I am still able to concentrate fully, but am more detached and less involved. In this position, I can make sensible decisions with regard to the counselling process. However, I can in a split second travel back in my imagination, to my counselling chair, to give empathic attention and empathic responses to the client. Clearly I have a powerful imagination, and have trained myself to relax quickly, when necessary. You will need to experiment for yourself, to devise an effective way in which you can protect yourself from emotional damage due to excessive exposure to client pain.

Despite the above discussion, there will inevitably be times when, as a counsellor, you *are* affected by the emotional traumas of your clients. Occasionally, it may be helpful for you to let your client know that you have been emotionally affected by what he has told you. Generally, though, you will need to control the expression of your own emotions appropriately, so that the client's needs are receiving full attention. If you are left in an emotionally disturbed state after a counselling session, then talk to your supervisor about your feelings as soon as possible.

The counselling relationship is substantially a one-way relationship, in which the counsellor is the giver and the client is the taker. Such a relationship inevitably drains the counsellor of emotional energy. Clearly, unless a counsellor recharges himself, he will experience the symptoms of burnout as he becomes drained.

It is important to be aware of the dangers of over-involvement with clients and their issues. We all have different personalities and differing capabilities for coping with emotionally stressful situations. Some counsellors get over-involved with their clients and take their client's problems home with them, whereas other people are more philosophical and are less affected by their counselling work. I have trained myself so that when I leave my place of work, I will allow myself to think about client material only until I reach a particular set of traffic lights. Once I have passed these lights, I give myself the option of going back to my place of work to think about clients, or of forgetting them and continuing my journey. I invariably continue my journey.

Experienced counsellors who deal with suicidal or violent clients have an extremely stressful time and are particularly prone to burnout. It is likely that a counsellor who has a high case-load of suicidal clients may eventually have to accept that one of his clients has succeeded in killing himself. This knowledge creates anxiety in the counsellor and may increase the likelihood of burnout. Remember that ultimately only the client can be responsible for his decision. It is not appropriate to blame yourself for what you cannot prevent. Protect yourself, as a new counsellor, by ensuring that such clients are referred for appropriate professional help.

Being isolated and working alone puts a counsellor at increased risk of burnout, because of a lack of peer support during the working day. After all, if I'm being drained of my energy, I need to be able to get some back by interacting with others who can meet with me in equal two-way relationships.

It has been suggested by some that stress to the counsellor in his personal life may make him more susceptible to burnout. However, I have not found any evidence to confirm this view, although it may be true. My guess is that some people are more susceptible to burnout than others.

As stated before, many counsellors are afraid to admit to themselves, let alone to other people, that they are starting to experience burnout symptoms, because they feel that it would be an admission of failure. This is understandable for many reasons. Firstly, we have all learnt from childhood to appear to be strong enough to cope with our load whatever that may be. That learning is based on a myth that human beings are inexhaustible, which is obviously not true. Secondly, new counsellors invariably start counselling with very high ideals and unrealistically high expectations of what they will be able to achieve.

My own experience as a counsellor is that usually the outcomes of counselling interventions give me satisfaction. However, there are times when a client does not seem to be helped by the counselling process and when this does happen, it would be easy for me to become disillusioned. At times like this I remind myself of the need for me to look at the overall picture. Outcomes with clients are often different from what the counsellor would prefer, and it is therefore necessary to have realistic expectations in order to avoid disillusionment. The idealism of the new counsellor can easily be eroded and lead to later dissatisfaction if unrealistic expectations are not fulfilled.

Giving with no expectation of return, caring for people unconditionally, and being dedicated to counselling work, are all attitudes which are implicitly absorbed as part of most counsellor training programs. These attitudes conflict strongly with feelings which may be experienced during burnout. It is therefore not surprising that counsellors find it difficult to own burnout feelings.

It is strongly recommended that counsellor training programs always include education for trainee counsellors about the inevitability of burnout occurring, at times, even in the most dedicated counsellor. If counsellors realize that burnout feelings do occur in normal, competent, capable and caring counsellors, then they will be able to start accepting their own burnout feelings and to share those feelings with their peers and other professionals.

Burnout comes in cycles and it is helpful to expect these cycles to occur. It is healthy to say "Ah-ha, I'm starting to recognize some of the symptoms of burnout". By making that simple statement, a counsellor is able to admit truthfully what is happening and is then empowered to take the necessary action to deal with the problem.

Most counsellors start their job with some feelings of nervousness, but very soon this is followed by enthusiasm and excitement. However, it doesn't take long for other feelings to set in. These may be feelings of stagnation and apathy, or even of frustration and annoyance. In other words, the counsellor's initial enthusiasm and excitement will, from time to time, be replaced by feelings which are associated with burnout. In the same way, by using sensible burnout management techniques, the initial enthusiasm about counselling can be re-experienced.

Experiencing burnout is not a disaster if it is recognized and dealt with effectively. Dealing with burnout is no more difficult for the counsellor than servicing a car is for the car owner. Once you become aware of your burnout feelings, take the appropriate action to recharge yourself, to regain your enthusiasm and the excitement which you experienced at the beginning of your counselling career. This can be done time and again, and so you can work as a counsellor for a lifetime if you choose by recharging yourself and starting afresh from time to time.

Quite often people look for a new job or resign as a result of burnout. That is one way of dealing with it, but it is not necessary to do that if you recognize the symptoms early enough and do something positive to deal with them. Recognizing and owning burnout seems to be a problem for many counsellors, so to help in identifying burnout in its early stages I have devised a burnout inventory known as the Geldard Burnout Inventory, or the GBI. A copy of the GBI, with instructions for use, is included in Chapter 28. Use it to check your own burnout level from time to time.

Here are some suggestions for dealing with burnout.

1. Recognize and own the symptoms.
2. Talk with someone about your feelings.
3. Re-schedule your work.
4. Cut down on your workload.
5. Take a holiday.
6. Use relaxation or meditation.
7. Use positive self-talk.
8. Lower your expectations of yourself.
9. Lower your expectations of your clients.
10. Lower your expectations of your peers.
11. Lower your expectations of your employer.
12. Allow yourself to enjoy life and have a sense of humour.
13. Use thought-stopping to stop worrying about clients when not at work.
14. Use your religious or other belief system for support.

Some of these ideas will now be discussed further. Firstly, it is interesting to note that simply admitting that you are experiencing burnout will affect your behaviour and enable you to cope better. Talking with your supervisor or someone else may also be helpful, as by doing this you may more easily be able to clarify your options with regard to suitable methods of intervention.

It can be helpful to re-schedule your work so that you have a feeling of being in control. You may need to be assertive with your boss if he doesn't understand your need for a reasonable workload. Reducing your workload may not be sufficient initially, and you may need to take a few days off, to have a holiday, or to take some days off sick. Help yourself to feel more relaxed, more in control and fitter. Build into your lifestyle proper times for rest, recreation, exercise, light-hearted relief and relaxation. Doing relaxation exercises or meditating can be helpful. Use positive self-talk to replace negative self-statements and challenge the negative self-statements you make about others. This involves changing your expectations of yourself, your clients and your peers.

A useful way to deal with burnout is to take a less severe view of life, to allow yourself to have a sense of humour, and to be less intense in your work. Be carefree and have fun. Most important, do not take client problems home. If you do catch yourself doing this, practise thought-stopping. The first step in thought-stopping is to recognize that you are thinking about client problems when you should be relaxing. Then recognize your choice, to continue thinking about these problems or to focus your attention on something in your present environment. This may involve doing something physical or it may involve concentrating on something specific such as listening to music. Focus all your energy and attention on the here-and-now to block out the intruding thoughts. Sometimes you may find that the intruding thoughts recur and that you catch yourself saying "If I don't think about this client problem now, then I will never deal with it and that will be bad for the client". If such a thought comes into your mind, then fix a time at your place of work when you will deal with that issue, and say to yourself, "OK at 10 o'clock tomorrow morning, I will devote half an hour to thinking about that problem, but right now I will get on with doing and thinking about things that are pleasant for me".

Many counsellors find strength in their religious beliefs and gain through prayer and meditation. They find that by doing this they receive an inner strength which enables them to be more effective in their work. Similarly, people with other philosophical belief systems can use their philosophy of life as an aid in combatting burnout.

Be assured that if you care for yourself, and take appropriate action to attend to your own needs by leading a less pressured and more balanced life, then your burnout symptoms will fade and you will be able to regain your energy and enthusiasm. However, if you are like most counsellors, you will have an ongoing struggle with burnout which will come and go. There will always be times when you will give too much of yourself, and then need to redress the balance so that your own needs for recharging are adequately met.

Further reading on burnout

Edelwich, J. and Brodsky, A. *Burnout: Stages of Disillusionment in the Helping Professions.* New York: Human Sciences, 1980.

Farber, B. A. *Stress and Burnout in the Human Service Professions.* New York: 1983.

Freudenberger, H. J. and Richelson, G. *Burnout: The High Cost of High Achievement.* Sydney: Bantam, 1981.

Maslach, C. *Burnout: The Cost of Caring.* Englewood Cliffs: Prentice Hall, 1982.

Pines, A., Aronston, E. and Kafry, D. *Burnout: From Tedium to Personal Growth.* New York: Free Press, 1981.

Veninga, R. L. and Spradley, J. P. *The Work/Stress Connection: How to Cope with Job Burnout.* Boston: Little/Brown, 1981.

28 The Geldard Burnout Inventory

The Geldard Burnout Inventory (GBI) can be used as an indication of burnout level, but more importantly it can be used in a qualitative way by the counsellor himself as he fills it in. If you do the inventory yourself, after you have completed it, go back through the questions and decide for yourself whether your answers suggest that you are starting to become jaded, exhausted, disillusioned and generally burnt out.

A copy of the GBI follows, at the end of which are instructions for scoring and interpretation.

The Geldard Burnout Inventory

Answer this inventory by putting an "X" over the appropriate "I" on each rating scale as shown in the example below. Please put each "X" over an "I" and not at intermediate points.

For example:

Strongly   Disagree   Mildly   Don't   Mildly   Agree   Strongly
disagree   disagree know   agree   agree
  I --------I--------I--------I--------I--------X--------I

"X" here means "Agree"_____↑

1. I have positive attitudes to counselling and think that the work is really worthwhile.

Strongly   Disagree   Mildly   Don't   Mildly   Agree   Strongly
disagree   disagree know   agree   agree
  I --------I--------I--------I--------I--------I--------I

2. There is too much to do in a day.

Strongly   Disagree   Mildly   Don't   Mildly   Agree   Strongly
disagree   disagree know   agree   agree
  I --------I--------I--------I--------I--------I--------I

187

3. I always relate to clients on a personal and individual basis, and do not treat them just as cases to be dealt with.

Strongly disagree	Disagree	Mildly disagree	Don't know	Mildly agree	Agree	Strongly agree
I -------- I -------- I -------- I -------- I -------- I -------- I

4. I am always willing to do extra work.

Strongly disagree	Disagree	Mildly disagree	Don't know	Mildly agree	Agree	Strongly agree
I -------- I -------- I -------- I -------- I -------- I -------- I

5. My personal life is suffering as a result of my counselling work.

Strongly disagree	Disagree	Mildly disagree	Don't know	Mildly agree	Agree	Strongly agree
I -------- I -------- I -------- I -------- I -------- I -------- I

6. I feel as though I need to hide my inadequacies and faults.

Strongly disagree	Disagree	Mildly disagree	Don't know	Mildly agree	Agree	Strongly agree
I -------- I -------- I -------- I -------- I -------- I -------- I

7. When I go home I usually forget about my clients and get on with the rest of my life.

Strongly disagree	Disagree	Mildly disagree	Don't know	Mildly agree	Agree	Strongly agree
I -------- I -------- I -------- I -------- I -------- I -------- I

8. I don't blame clients for their problems. Mostly they can't help themselves. They are victims of society and need ongoing support and help.

Strongly disagree	Disagree	Mildly disagree	Don't know	Mildly agree	Agree	Strongly agree
I -------- I -------- I -------- I -------- I -------- I -------- I

9. I usually look forward with pleasant anticipation to clients coming.

Strongly disagree	Disagree	Mildly disagree	Don't know	Mildly agree	Agree	Strongly agree
I -------- I -------- I -------- I -------- I -------- I -------- I

10. I can't do the job the way I think is best. There are too many don'ts.

Strongly   Disagree   Mildly   Don't   Mildly   Agree   Strongly
disagree   disagree know   agree   agree
I -------- I -------- I -------- I -------- I -------- I -------- I

11. The system at work needs changing, but I haven't the power to change it.

Strongly   Disagree   Mildly   Don't   Mildly   Agree   Strongly
disagree   disagree know   agree   agree
I -------- I -------- I -------- I -------- I -------- I -------- I

12. I often feel like saying to clients: "You think you have problems; what about me?"

Strongly   Disagree   Mildly   Don't   Mildly   Agree   Strongly
disagree   disagree know   agree   agree
I -------- I -------- I -------- I -------- I -------- I -------- I

13. I find it easy to talk to other counsellors about my feelings.

Strongly   Disagree   Mildly   Don't   Mildly   Agree   Strongly
disagree   disagree know   agree   agree
I -------- I -------- I -------- I -------- I -------- I -------- I

14. I feel emotionally depleted.

Strongly   Disagree   Mildly   Don't   Mildly   Agree   Strongly
disagree   disagree know   agree   agree
I -------- I -------- I -------- I -------- I -------- I -------- I

15. I just can't cope with some types of client.

Strongly   Disagree   Mildly   Don't   Mildly   Agree   Strongly
disagree   disagree know   agree   agree
I -------- I -------- I -------- I -------- I -------- I -------- I

16. I feel as though I am losing the ability to get in touch with some clients' feelings.

Strongly   Disagree   Mildly   Don't   Mildly   Agree   Strongly
disagree   disagree know   agree   agree
I -------- I -------- I -------- I -------- I -------- I -------- I

17. Counselling is all giving with no return.

Strongly disagree	Disagree	Mildly disagree	Don't know	Mildly agree	Agree	Strongly agree
I -------- I -------- I -------- I -------- I -------- I -------- I

18. People hold counsellors in high regard.

Strongly disagree	Disagree	Mildly disagree	Don't know	Mildly agree	Agree	Strongly agree
I -------- I -------- I -------- I -------- I -------- I -------- I

19. Many clients deserve to suffer because they just don't live by decent moral standards.

Strongly disagree	Disagree	Mildly disagree	Don't know	Mildly agree	Agree	Strongly agree
I -------- I -------- I -------- I -------- I -------- I -------- I

20. I really need to take a break from counselling.

Strongly disagree	Disagree	Mildly disagree	Don't know	Mildly agree	Agree	Strongly agree
I -------- I -------- I -------- I -------- I -------- I -------- I

21. I feel warm and friendly towards my fellow counsellors.

Strongly disagree	Disagree	Mildly disagree	Don't know	Mildly agree	Agree	Strongly agree
I -------- I -------- I -------- I -------- I -------- I -------- I

22. I believe that my standard of counselling is improving.

Strongly disagree	Disagree	Mildly disagree	Don't know	Mildly agree	Agree	Strongly agree
I -------- I -------- I -------- I -------- I -------- I -------- I

23. My relationship with clients is suffering due to my negative attitudes.

Strongly disagree	Disagree	Mildly disagree	Don't know	Mildly agree	Agree	Strongly agree
I -------- I -------- I -------- I -------- I -------- I -------- I

24. I often feel angry when I hear what the client has done.

| Strongly disagree | Disagree | Mildly disagree | Don't know | Mildly agree | Agree | Strongly agree |

I -------- I -------- I -------- I -------- I -------- I -------- I

25. I feel physically fit and have lots of energy.

| Strongly disagree | Disagree | Mildly disagree | Don't know | Mildly agree | Agree | Strongly agree |

I -------- I -------- I -------- I -------- I -------- I -------- I

26. Clients are forever grasping, self-centred and unappreciative of my efforts.

| Strongly disagree | Disagree | Mildly disagree | Don't know | Mildly agree | Agree | Strongly agree |

I -------- I -------- I -------- I -------- I -------- I -------- I

27. Counselling gives me a lift in life and inspires me to move forwards.

| Strongly disagree | Disagree | Mildly disagree | Don't know | Mildly agree | Agree | Strongly agree |

I -------- I -------- I -------- I -------- I -------- I -------- I

28. I haven't enough energy left for my family and friends. Counselling takes too much of me.

| Strongly disagree | Disagree | Mildly disagree | Don't know | Mildly agree | Agree | Strongly agree |

I -------- I -------- I -------- I -------- I -------- I -------- I

29. I feel worn out by the people who come in.

| Strongly disagree | Disagree | Mildly disagree | Don't know | Mildly agree | Agree | Strongly agree |

I -------- I -------- I -------- I -------- I -------- I -------- I

30. I can't let off steam in my counselling workplace. I've got to be calm, patient and caring all of the time.

| Strongly disagree | Disagree | Mildly disagree | Don't know | Mildly agree | Agree | Strongly agree |

I -------- I -------- I -------- I -------- I -------- I -------- I

31. I feel enthusiastic about the value of counselling.

Strongly disagree	Disagree	Mildly disagree	Don't know	Mildly agree	Agree	Strongly agree
I -------- I -------- I -------- I -------- I -------- I -------- I

32. I often get caught up in the clients' emotional feelings and feel upset or angry myself.

Strongly disagree	Disagree	Mildly disagree	Don't know	Mildly agree	Agree	Strongly agree
I -------- I -------- I -------- I -------- I -------- I -------- I

33. I often wish the client would just go away.

Strongly disagree	Disagree	Mildly disagree	Don't know	Mildly agree	Agree	Strongly agree
I -------- I -------- I -------- I -------- I -------- I -------- I

34. I know what my supervisor thinks of my performance as a counsellor.

Strongly disagree	Disagree	Mildly disagree	Don't know	Mildly agree	Agree	Strongly agree
I -------- I -------- I -------- I -------- I -------- I -------- I

35. The agency I work for really cares about me and my work there is appreciated.

Strongly disagree	Disagree	Mildly disagree	Don't know	Mildly agree	Agree	Strongly agree
I -------- I -------- I -------- I -------- I -------- I -------- I

36. I get a hopeless feeling. Nobody can fix up all the problems out there.

Strongly disagree	Disagree	Mildly disagree	Don't know	Mildly agree	Agree	Strongly agree
I -------- I -------- I -------- I -------- I -------- I -------- I

37. I hardly ever give automatic type responses.

Strongly disagree	Disagree	Mildly disagree	Don't know	Mildly agree	Agree	Strongly agree
I -------- I -------- I -------- I -------- I -------- I -------- I

38. Counselling has given me the satisfaction that I originally expected to get from it.

Strongly disagree	Disagree	Mildly disagree	Don't know	Mildly agree	Agree	Strongly agree
I -------- I -------- I -------- I -------- I -------- I -------- I

39. I feel irritable quite often.

Strongly disagree	Disagree	Mildly disagree	Don't know	Mildly agree	Agree	Strongly agree
I -------- I -------- I -------- I -------- I -------- I -------- I

40. I rarely feel uptight.

Strongly disagree	Disagree	Mildly disagree	Don't know	Mildly agree	Agree	Strongly agree
I -------- I -------- I -------- I -------- I -------- I -------- I

Instructions for scoring and interpreting the GBI

Each item on the GBI receives a score from 1 to 7. The following items are scored in the same way. Items 1, 3, 4, 7, 8, 9, 13, 18, 21, 22, 25, 27, 31, 34, 35, 37, 38, and 40, score as follows:

Strongly disagree	7
Disagree	6
Mildly disagree	5
Don't know	4
Mildly agree	3
Agree	2
Strongly agree	1

Thus scoring is as follows:

Strongly disagree	Disagree	Mildly disagree	Don't know	Mildly agree	Agree	Strongly agree
I -------- I -------- I -------- I -------- I -------- I -------- I
7	6	5	4	3	2	1

Items 2, 5, 6, 10, 11, 12, 14, 15, 16, 17, 19, 20, 23, 24, 26, 28, 29, 30, 32, 33, 36, 39 are all scored in the following way:

Strongly disagree   1
Disagree   2
Mildly disagree   3
Don't know   4
Mildly agree   5
Agree   6
Strongly agree   7

Thus scoring is as follows:

Strongly disagree	Disagree	Mildly disagree	Don't know	Mildly agree	Agree	Strongly agree
I -------- I -------- I -------- I -------- I -------- I -------- I
1	2	3	4	5	6	7

Write the score for each item on the right hand side of the page against that item. In order to obtain your total burnout score, add together the scores for all items. Use the following key to interpret your result.

Key

SCORE	INTERPRETATION
40–80	You are a fully functioning counsellor
81–120	You're doing well
121–200	Why not give yourself more caring? You deserve to be loved. Love yourself!
201–280	Urgent action needed! Your burnout score is too high.

References

Bandler, R. *Using Your Brain for a CHANGE—Neuro-Linguistic Programming.* Moab: Real People Press, 1985.

Bandler, R. and Grinder, J. *Frogs into Princes: Neuro-Linguistic Programming.* Moab: Real People Press, 1979.

Bandler, R., Grinder, J. and Satir, V. *Changing with Families.* Palo Alto: Science and Behavior Books, 1976.

Bandler, R. and Grinder, J. *Reframing—Neuro-Linguistic Programming and the Transformation of Meaning.* Moab: Real People Press, 1982.

Benjamin, A. *The Helping Interview.* Boston: Houghton Mifflin, 1982.

Berent, I. *The Algebra of Suicide.* New York: Human Sciences, 1981.

Bernard, M. E. *Staying Rational in an Irrational World.* Melbourne: Macmillan, 1986.

Bernstein, D. A. and Borkovec, T. D. *Progressive Relaxation Training: A Manual for the Helping Professions.* Illinois: Research Press, 1973.

Berne, E. *Games People Play.* Harmondsworth: Penguin, 1964.

Brammer, L. M. *The Helping Relationship—Process and Skills.* Englewood Cliffs: Prentice Hall, 1988 (fourth edition).

Brammer, L. M., Shostrom, E. L. and Abrego, P. *Therapeutic Psychology Fundamentals of Counseling and Psychotherapy.* Englewood Cliffs: Prentice Hall, 1988 (fifth edition).

Brenner, D. *The Effective Therapist.* New York: Pergamon, 1982.

Brown, D. and Srebalus, D. J. *An Introduction to the Counseling Profession.* Englewood Cliffs: Prentice Hall, 1988.

Burns, D. D. *Feeling Good—The New Mood Therapy.* New York: Signet, 1980.

Cameron-Bandler, L. and Lebeau, M. *The Emotional Hostage—Rescuing Your Emotional Life.* San Rafael: FuturePace, 1986.

Combs, A. and Avila, D. *Helping Relationships: Basic Concepts for the Helping Professions.* Newton: Allyn & Bacon, 1985.

Corey, G., Corey, C. and Callanan, P. *Issues and Ethics in the Helping Professions.* Monterey: Brooks/Cole, 1982.

Cormier, L. S. and Hackney, H. *The Professional Counselor—A Process Guide to Helping.* Englewood Cliffs: Prentice Hall, 1987.

Corsini, R. J. *Current Psychotherapies.* Itasca: Peacock, 1979.

Cox, M. *Structuring the Therapeutic Process—Compromise with Chaos.* Oxford: Pergamon, 1978.

Dixon, D. N. and Glover, J. A. *Counseling—A Problem Solving Approach.* New York: Wiley, 1984.

Dunne, E. J., McIntosh, J. L. and Dunne-Maxim, K. (eds). *Suicide and its Aftermath: Understanding and Counseling the Survivors.* New York: Norton, 1987.

Dyer, W. W. *Your Erroneous Zones.* London: Sphere, 1976.

Edelwich, J. and Brodsky, A. *Burnout: Stages of Disillusionment in the Helping Professions.* New York: Human Sciences, 1980.

Egan, G. *The Skilled Helper.* Monterey: Brooks/Cole, 1975.

Ellis, A. and Bernard, M.E. (eds). *Clinical Applications of Rational-Emotive Therapy.* New York: Plenum, 1975.

Ellis, A. and Harper, R. A. *A New Guide to Rational Living.* Hollywood: Wilshire Book Company, 1975.

Fabian, S. *The Last Taboo: Suicide and Attempted Suicide Among Children and Adolescents.* Ringwood, Penguin, 1986.

Farber, B. A. *Stress and Burnout in the Human Service Professions.* New York: Pergamon, 1983.

Farelly, F. and Brandsma, J. *Provocative Therapy.* California: Meta, 1982.

Feindler, E. L. *Adolescent Anger Control: Cognitive Behavioral Techniques.* New York: Pergamon, 1986.

Freudenberger, H. J. and Richelson, G. *Burnout: The High Cost of High Achievement.* Sydney: Bantam, 1981.

George, R. L. and Dustin, D. *Group Counselling—Theory and Practice.* Englewood Cliffs: Prentice Hall. 1988.

Gerber, S. K. *Responsive Therapy—A Systematic Approach to Counseling Skills.* New York: Human Sciences, 1986.

Glasser, W. *Reality Therapy.* New York: Harper Colophon, 1975.

Harris, T. A. *I'm OK—You're OK.* London: Pan, 1970.

Hawton, K. and Catalan, J. *Attempted Suicide: A Practical Guide to its Nature and Management.* Oxford: Oxford University Press, 1987.

Hendricks, G. *Learning to Love Yourself—A Guide to Becoming Centered.* Englewood Cliffs: Prentice Hall, 1982.

Hepworth, D. H. and Larsen, J. A. *Direct Social Work Practice Theory and Skills.* Illinois, Dorsey, 1982.

Howie, M. *Developing Helping Skills.* Melbourne: Skillington House, 1982.

Hutchins, D. E. and Cole, C. D. *Helping Relationships and Strategies.* Monterey: Brooks/Cole 1986.

Ivey, A. *Intentional Interviewing and Counseling.* Monterey: Brooks/Cole, 1983.

Ivey, A. E., Ivey, M. B. and Simek-Downing, L. *Counseling and Psychotherapy—Integrating Skills, Theory and Practice.* Englewood Cliffs: Prentice Hall, 1987.

Knutson, J. F. *The Control of Aggression.* Chicago: Aldine, 1973.

Kubler-Ross, E. *Death: The Final Stage of Growth.* Englewood Cliffs: Prentice Hall, 1975.

Lankton, S. R. *Practical Majic—A Translation of Basic Neuro-Linguistic Programming into Clinical Psychotherapy.* Cupertino: Meta, 1980.

Lester, G. and Lester, D. *Suicide: The Gamble With Death.* Englewood Cliffs: Prentice Hall, 1971.

Levine, S. *Meetings at the Edge—Dialogues with the Grieving and the Dying.* New York: Anchor, 1984.

Levine, S. *Who Dies? An Investigation of Conscious Living and Conscious Dying.* New York: Anchor, 1982.

Lewis, B. A. and Pucelik, R. F. *Majic Demystified—A Pragmatic Guide to Communication Change.* Oregon: Metamorphous, 1982.

Long, L., Paradise, L. and Long, T. *Questioning Skills for the Helping Process.* Monterey: Brooks/Cole, 1981.

Maslach, C. *Burnout: The Cost of Caring.* Englewood Cliffs: Prentice Hall, 1982.

Murgatroyd, S. *Counselling and Helping.* London: Methuen, 1985.

Novaco, R. W. *Anger Control.* Toronto: Lexington, 1975.

Parkes, C. M. *Bereavement: Studies of Grief in Adult Life.* Harmondsworth: Penguin, 1986.

Patterson, C. H. *Theories of Counseling and Psychotherapy.* New York: Harper & Rowe, 1986.

Pietrofesa, J., Hoffman, A. and Splete, H. H. *Counseling—An Introduction.* Boston: Houghton Mifflin, 1984.

Pines, A., Aronson, E. and Kafry, D. *Burnout: From Tedium to Personal Growth.* New York: Free Press, 1981.

Polster, E. and Polster, M. *Gestalt Therapy Integrated.* New York: Vintage, 1974.

Priestly, P. and McGuire, J. *Learning to Help—Basic Skills and Exercises.* London: Tavistock, 1983.

Rogers, C. R. *Client-Centered Therapy.* Boston: Houghton Mifflin, 1955.

Rogers, C. R. *On Becoming a Person—A Therapist's View of Psychotherapy.* London: Constable, 1961.

Satir, V. *Self Esteem.* Millbrae: Celestial Arts, 1975.

Shertzer, B., and Stone, S.C. *Fundamentals of Counseling.* Boston: Houghton Mifflin, 1974.

Stengel, E. *Suicide and Attempted Suicide.* Harmondsworth: Penguin, 1983.

Veninga, R. L. and Spradley, J. P. *The Work/Stress Connection: How to Cope with Job Burnout.* Boston: Little/Brown, 1981.

Wills, T. A. (ed). *Basic Processes in Helping Relationships.* New York: Academic Press, 1982.

Worden, J. W. *Grief Counselling and Grief Therapy.* London: Tavistock, 1986.

Zinker, J. *Creative Process in Gestalt Therapy.* New York: Vintage, 1977.

Index